Above the Gravel Bar

Above the Gravel Bar

The Native Canoe Routes of Maine

Third Edition

David S. Cook

With a Foreword by
James Eric Francis, Sr.
Tribal Historian of the Penobscot Nation

Introduction by
David Sanger
University of Maine, Orono

Polar Bear & Company
An imprint of the
Solon Center for Research and Publishing
Solon, Maine

Polar Bear & Company™
Solon Center for Research and Publishing
PO Box 311, Solon, ME 04979, U.S.A.
207.643.2795, polarbearandco.org, soloncenter.org

Copyright © 1985, 1999, 2007 by David S. Cook
All rights reserved. No part of this book may be reproduced in any form without permission in writing from the author or publisher, except for brief quotations for critical articles and reviews.
First edition 1985; Second edition 1999.
First printing of third edition April 2007; on demand from March 2017.
Cover: Emily Cornell du Houx. Illustrations: David S. Cook, p. 66, petroglyphs; Emily Cornell du Houx, David S. Cook, pp. ii, 32, 36, 39, 115; James Eric Francis, Sr., pp. ix, xiv; Herb Hartman, p. v; Mike Krepner, David S. Cook, Paul Cornell du Houx, based on maps by Native Trails, Inc., pp. 15, 57, 61, 71, 74, 82, 100; courtesy of Maine Department of Inland Fisheries and Wildlife, pp. 47, 49, 63.

Library of Congress Cataloging-in-Publication Data

Cook, David S. (David Sidney), 1943-
Above the gravel bar : the native canoe routes of Maine / by David S. Cook.
— 3rd ed.
p. cm.
Summary: "Native canoe routes of Maine, with translations of place names, are described in the context of Northeastern geological development and Indian prehistoric culture in the use of birch bark canoes on rivers, lakes, carries, and coastal routes, according to the archaeological and historical record, informed by accounts of early explorers"—Provided by publisher.
Includes bibliographical references and index.
ISBN-13: 978-1-882190-69-0 (alk. paper)
ISBN-10: 1-882190-69-6 (alk. paper)
1. Canoes and canoeing—Maine.
2. Indians of North America—Boats—Maine. I. Title.
GV776.M2C66 2006
797.1'2209741—dc22
2006029623

Manufactured on durable, acid-free paper in more than one country.

In memory of Myron S. Smart
1902–1984

Contents

List of Maps viii
Foreword ix
Introduction xv
Preface..xxi
1. With a Little Help from My Friends.............................1
2. Land and Water..16
3. The Canoes 21
4. Canoeing, Camping, Carrying and Castor canadensis......33
   Carries 40
   Castor canadensis 47
5. The Routes...51
   Canoeing in the Gulf of Maine 52
   Western Maine...56
   Mid-Coastal Canoe Routes 67
   Coastal Cutoffs.. 68
   The Penobscot System...70
   The St. John River 99
   The Allagash 109
   The Upper St. John... 112
6. The Canoe Routes Today....................................... 114
Notes 123
Bibliography..127
Index 131
The author 144

Maps

Maine and the Maritime Peninsula xxiv
Canoe Routes of Maine 15
by Marc Lescarbot 31
by John Mitchell 50
Androscoggin and Kennebec Rivers 57
Kennebec and Penobscot Routes to the St. Lawrence 61
Central Maine Coast 66
Penobscot River and the Downeast Coast 71
The Piscataquis Ahwangan 74
by Joseph Chadwick 77
The Maliseet Trail 82
Northern Canoe Routes 100

Foreword

We are the river. The river is us. It is in our veins. It is the absolute center of who we are as tribal people. —John Banks, tribal member and director of natural resources, Penobscot Nation

The Penobscot people, together with the Passamaquoddy, Micmac, and the Maliseet tribes, are collectively known as the Wabanaki, sharing a rich cultural heritage that spans thousands of years of Maine history.

The Penobscot River is the heart of Penobscot culture. The current of the river weaves back and forth in the landscape, exposing islands. Today these islands and the river represent the Penobscot Nation's reservation. Indian Island, the southernmost island, is the only one remaining that has year-round occupation. In the past, the river, the islands, and surrounding watershed provided the Penobscots with plant foods, game, medicine, and natural resources to make tools, shelter, and birchbark canoes.

Growing up on Indian Island I had a strong sense of culture and of place. Indian Island was our home, and the surrounding river sacred. As a youth, places like Joe Pease Rapids, Sandy Beach,

Fort Dawson, Down Street, and Oak Hill defined places on the reservation. Orson Island, Birch Island, Birch Stream, Hemlock Island, and Eber's Point were some of the places just off reservation that held importance for hunting, and gathering materials for basket making and other cultural activities. When very young, Indian Island defined my boundaries; my mother would often say, "Don't go over town."

"Over town" was Old Town, Maine, just across the bridge from Indian Island. It wasn't until I was in the seventh grade that I began to frequent Old Town more often. I attended Old Town High School. After graduation I joined the United States Air Force and found myself in Cheyenne, Wyoming. In Wyoming I got a profound feeling of displacement. This homesickness wasn't limited to my family, friends, and tribal members; I missed the landscape. Wyoming, seemingly devoid of trees and rivers, was a foreign landscape to me. After a four-year tour, I returned home to Maine.

In Maine I attended the University of Maine at Orono and studied my true passion, *History*. One day in a Native American Studies class, we learned about the Trail of Tears. Thoughts of how out of place I felt in Cheyenne fueled my empathy for the Cherokee who where displaced from their homeland, the land that for generations they lived in concert with. They were forcibly moved to another land unfamiliar to them, hundreds of miles away. Native American cultures rely on the landscape for many aspects of their culture. To be displaced to another landscape, an unfamiliar landscape, is devastating to that culture. The fact that they survived in that new landscape is a testament to their strength and adaptability. Walking across the campus that day in the shadow of the pine trees, I realized that Penobscots are still in their ancestral homeland. It was on that day that I began looking at the landscape differently.

To truly understand Penobscot history, you must understand the ancestral landscape. The Penobscot ancestral territory wasn't limited to the Penobscot River valley. Land from the Machias River in the east to Cape Ann in Massachusetts defined the ancestral territory of the Penobscot Nation. The Machias, Union, Kennebec, Androscoggin, Royal, Presumpscot, Saco, and Piscataqua river basins were occupied by the ancestors of the Penobscot Nation. By the twentieth century, Penobscots were limited to the Penobscot River, from shore to shore, and the islands in the river.

During the eighteenth and nineteenth centuries, many surveyors and explorers hired Penobscot guides because of their knowledge of the landscape. In the 1830s Joseph Treat hired John Neptune as a guide on a journey that took them up the Penobscot River to the Allagash River, on to the St. John River, portaging to the Mattawamkeag, and back to the Penobscot River. Later in the late 1840s and early 1850s, Henry David Thoreau visited Maine on three occasions. For his second trip he hired Joseph Attean as his guide. They left Bangor and traveled to Greenville by coach. They then paddled the length of Moosehead Lake, portaged across Northeast Carry to the Penobscot River and to Chesuncook Lake and then returned. On Thoreau's third visit he hired the services of Joe Polis. Joe took Thoreau on a similar journey but continued down the East Branch of the Penobscot River and then traveled south on the main branch of the river to Indian Island. It is clear in the writing of both Thoreau and Treat that the guide had a vast knowledge of the waterways, portages, flora and fauna. The guides also shared *Indian* place names with their clients.

While I was in college, I transcribed many of the Indian place names and compiled them into map form. I drew a map of the entire Penobscot River from Verona Island to Nicatou Island at the fork of the east and west branches of the river. My research included Treat and Thoreau, but also included Fanny Hardy Eckstorm's *Indian Place Names of the Penobscot Valley and the Maine Coast*. Eckstorm's book was extremely valuable because she had done extensive research on Indian place names. When I was finished I had a series of maps showing the river, streams, and islands labeled with the Indian place names. While transcribing what each place meant, it became clear that the place name holds an abundance of information about the Native American culture and the landscape. I was looking at a window into the past.

The Euro-American way to name a place is either by naming after someone, or naming for another place. For instance, Orono,

Maine, is named after a Penobscot chief from the late sixteenth century but is a Euro-American way to name a place. Penobscots had three basic ways of naming a particular location. Places were named for their geography or geology, the resources found there, or their names are based on legends that were passed down from generation to generation.

In Maine and the Maritimes, the rivers, lakes, streams, and ponds make a vast network to travel upon. The birchbark canoe was the primary vehicle in which to travel. Penobscots have had a sophisticated knowledge of the landscape and the resources found there. With this knowledge they traveled across the landscape, using water courses, to obtain food and other resources at the appropriate time of year. Geographic place names, like Passadumkeag which means "above the gravel bar," are clear markers for Native Americans traveling across the landscape. Today some of these place names remain in the Penobscot form, such as Passadumkeag, Kenduskeag, Mattawamkeag, and Penobscot; others have taken the meaning of the words and converted them into English. Stillwater, a branch of the Penobscot River, is derived from a description meaning "deadwater." Birch Stream and Hemlock Island and Stream are resource-based place names that have been converted to English.

Resource-based place names show us the importance of a particular resource in a particular place. Olamon Island, which means "red clay island," is a resource-based place name. The Passagassawassakeag River in Belfast means "where we speared sturgeon by torchlight." This activity and resource was so important to that place that it was named accordingly. This river is just off Penobscot Bay where we find a few place names attributed to legends.

There is an ancient Penobscot story about Gluskabe and the moose. In this story, after slaying the cow moose, Gluskabe chases a calf to Penobscot Bay. At the bay, Gluskabe kills the calf and throws the entrails and liver to his dog. Today, the location where Gluskabe killed the calf is known as Cape Rosier, but historically Penobscots knew it as the "moose rump." The liver and the entrails are also names on the landscape and act as markers for portage routes in the Penobscot Bay area. The liver, a large reddish-colored rock, is a marker showing an important portage route, so paddlers could avoid the dangerous wind near Cape Rosier. The entrails, which are located on Islesboro Island, are made of a white quartz stone. This large stone can be seen for several miles across Penobscot Bay, the white showing clearly against the dark surroundings. The rock is directly adjacent to a portage route bisecting Islesboro Island. It is clear that these "entrails" were used as a beacon to guide canoeists across the bay to an important portage.

Above the Gravel Bar, by David S. Cook, was another important book when understanding the ancestral landscape of the Penobscots. This book compiles the important canoe routes linking one basin/watershed to another. This information expands the extent of the knowledge of the landscape beyond a single river and puts the true ancestral landscape into perspective.

James Eric Francis, Sr.
Tribal Historian
Penobscot Nation

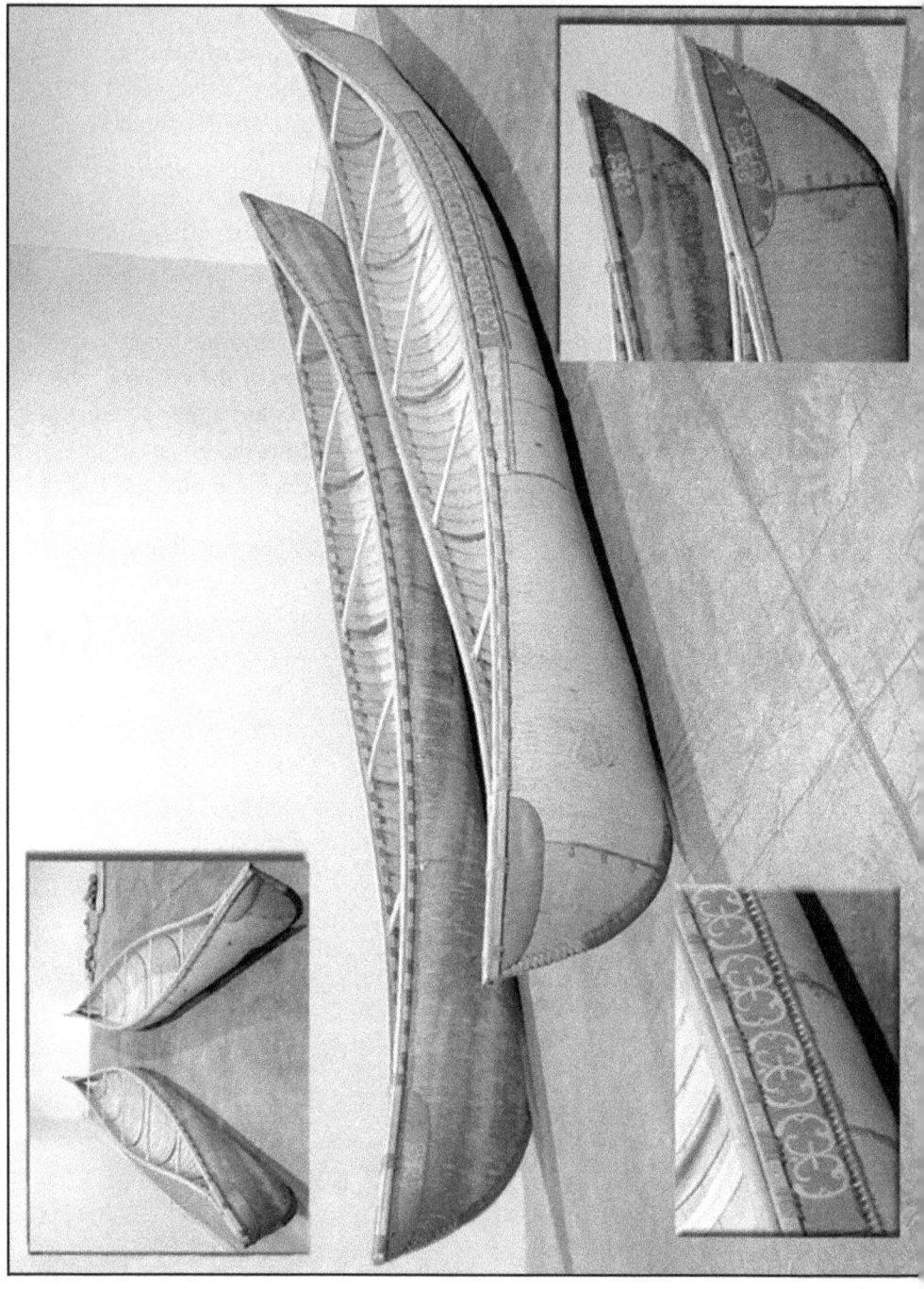

Introduction

Above the Gravel Bar is a masterful account of canoeing Maine's interconnected waterways. The author skillfully brings together his love of canoeing with a fascination for how the Native people utilized their watercraft to access even the remotest corners of Maine. In the absence of permanent villages, for these hunters, fishers, and gatherers, travel was a necessity of life, not recreation. As Dave Cook points out, there was no one to drive them to the headwaters of a waterway for a leisurely float downriver; for Native people canoeing meant going both upstream and downstream to access the land and its resources.

How ancient was this way of life? To answer this question we need to know something about the history of canoes in Maine and the Northeast. Obviously, the craft had to match the environment and available building materials. This leads to the question: what is known about birch tree distribution and past environmental conditions, and how might that have affected canoe use? Finally, in a region where water travel appears to have been so advantageous, how does this affect archaeological site selection?

A History of Canoes

Sixteenth and seventeenth century visitors to North America expressed their admiration for the competence of birchbark canoes and their skillful operators. Native people literally paddled circles around the clumsy, planked European craft. It soon became apparent that if the Europeans were going to penetrate far into the interior of the continent, they needed to adopt the birchbark as their vessel of choice, and they did.[1] Because of birchbark availability and the terrain, Canada was the hearth of the birchbark canoe. Maine lay on the periphery, which paralleled the distribution of paper birch (*Betula papyrifera*) large enough to provide the requisite big birchbark sheets. Other barks could form canoes, but none had the paper birch qualities.[2] In recognition of the superior traits of birchbarks, tribes who lived just south of the paper birch line often traded with their northern neighbors. When the French navigator Samuel de Champlain coasted west along Maine's coast in 1605, he noted the changeover from birchbark canoes to dugouts in northern Massachusetts; he commented on the dugouts' inherent instability.[3] Many archaeologists assert that at one time all of Maine and the Maritime Provinces was dugout canoe country. Is this reasonable, and what is the evidence?

As Dave Cook and others have pointed out, carrying a heavy dugout canoe around Maine rapids would present major challenges. Maine boasts no dugouts definitely dating to the pre-European era. The majority of old archaeological specimens come from Newnan's Lake in central Florida, where they date to several millennia BC.[4] Dating dugouts accurately depends on a radiocarbon analysis of the wood, which tells us only the age of that part of the tree, not the actual manufacturing date, a not-so-subtle point frequently overlooked. While we will probably never know when, where, or how often the birchbark canoe was invented, it is not farfetched to assume that any successful adaptation to the rapids-filled rivers of northern North America almost certainly mandated the use of the birchbark canoe, or something its equivalent. We do know from archaeological evidence that people had settled this vast area for over 8,000 years. Useful design modifications would have spread rapidly from one tribe to another, making any claim for the first example highly speculative. As with most indispensable items, Native traditionalists are likely to credit a supernatural gift.[5]

A submerged, white oak dugout recovered from Savannah Lake, Ohio, radiocarbon dated to about 3,500 years ago, old enough to hypothesize a Native American origin.[6] The authors of the study, an archaeologist and an engineer, calculated that the waterlogged canoe weighed about 1,000 pounds. In a dry state it would have a mass of about 700 pounds. Try carrying that around a set of rapids! From its size, they estimated a capacity of no more than four people, or a total capacity of about 1,500 pounds, assuming a freeboard of only four inches. How would it have functioned in the ocean or a large lake? Given the rounded hull shape of eastern seaboard dugouts, and lack of an outrigger, they must be ballasted heavily in order to achieve much stability, further reducing freeboard. The flat nature of their profile would further limit their ability to take on even a modest sea. The point is that from a purely functional viewpoint, when negotiating the waterways of the north, dugout canoes could only have been used on rivers with little drop, and under calm, wetland and protected estuarine conditions. On occasion, archaeologists and filmmakers evoke the storied dugout canoes of the Northwest Coast people, conjuring up images of similar craft cruising along the coast of Maine. The comparison is totally inappropriate.[7]

Stone gouges, reminiscent of modern steel gouges, are common in Maine and the Maritime Provinces during what archaeologists call the Archaic period, roughly 9,500 to 3,000 years ago. Northeastern archaeologists often take it for granted that gouges functioned to fashion dugout canoes.[8] Burning, followed by scraping, was the universal manufacturing method all down the eastern seaboard.[9] Interestingly, nowhere in the world where dugouts were being made in historic times do we find gouges in use. Gouges could have made dugouts, but there is no credible evidence supporting the belief, despite the common assertion in books and museum exhibits.

Historic accounts in the Northeast refer to moosehide boats, often used as expediency craft.[10] Apparently inferior to birchbark, logically they could have been a forerunner; however, the reverse could also hold. Simple evolutionary thinking on such matters can prove misleading. By historic times, birchbark canoes occurred in a wide variety of shapes and sizes, from the Mackenzie River drainage in the west, east to Newfoundland.[11] Some were lightweight and handy in rapid waters, while large, seagoing canoes permitted historically documented voyages over considerable distances.[12] When anthropologists see such diversity, they tend to suspect a substantial time depth, although it cannot be proven. Archaeological evidence indicates that people lived in the realm of birchbark canoes for over 10,000 years in some places, and, while it cannot demonstrated archaeologically that birchbark canoes existed over that long period of time, they could have, given the terrain and the obvious suitability of the craft. In short, there is no compelling reason to suspect that it was an invention (or a gift) of just the last few millennia.

Past Environments and Humans

Maine's Native peoples depended on the rivers and their canoes to access their homeland's resources. However, the waterways were not always as we see them today. Recent research has demonstrated that the rivers, lakes and other wetlands of the past few centuries differed from an earlier time. People first entered Maine sometime around 12,000 years ago (the actual date remains speculative), during a time when the melting icecaps contributed to high water levels in rivers and lakes. Shortly thereafter, drainage patterns changed.[13] Water levels dropped in response to increased aridity and warmer temperature, reaching an all-time low around 4,500 years ago. Then water levels began to rise again, and attained their highest point just about the time Europeans arrived.[14] Thus, canoeing would have been at its very best in the few centuries leading up to the modern era. Lowered water levels would have affected a number of biotic systems, including limiting fish habitats, as well as the ability of Native people to access the hinterlands reached by canoeists in recent times.[15]

According to paleo-botanists, paper birch has been growing in Maine throughout most of the last 10,000 years. Fossil evidence in the form of radiocarbon-dated paper birch catkin scales has been recovered from muddy sediments in a number of Maine ponds.[16]

Research has shown that during much of the Archaic period people lived in and around the lower reaches of Maine's major rivers. We find many sites on the banks of rivers, well situated to take advantage of the wetlands that dominate central and eastern Maine. Today, many of these are peat bogs which contain few resources of much interest to people. However, in the past, some of these peat bogs were open bodies of water with cattails and other edible plants.[17] In addition, the marshes would have supported beaver, muskrat, birds, fish, and amphibians, as well as attracting moose and deer, the remains of which all occur in archaeological sites.[18]

Site Locations

Although there are parts of the Northeast where Native people routinely established settlements well removed from navigable waterways, Maine was an exception. Systematic site surveys away from water rarely reveal pre-European archaeological sites, and those that do exist indicate a very special purpose, such as gathering rocks for tool making. With the exception of some very early sites—known as "Paleo-Indian" sites—in landscapes that are quite different in many ways, out of thousands of known site localities, only a handful are not beside a waterway accessible by a birchbark canoe. Part of this stems from the fact that a lightweight canoe can carry a huge cargo relative to a backpack. Even poling upstream, travel by canoe, as Dave Cook notes, was much easier and probably faster than striking off over land. Therefore, it should come as no surprise that once people had birchbark canoes they became the vehicle of choice.

After many years of research, we can recognize ideal campsite locations. Dave Cook indicates that one doesn't just camp anywhere along a riverbank, and neither did the Native people. A number of years ago, while addressing members of the press at a Penobscot River site, a reporter asked me why people camped here. After I had recited a number of obvious attractions, the somewhat incredulous response was, "just like us."

Native people lived along the coast of Maine for millennia, taking advantage of the littoral zone and also of the more open or pelagic ocean resources, such as swordfish which, incidentally, I cannot imagine being taken from traditional east-coast dugouts.[19] Coastal site locations suffer terribly from erosion, which means that our current site list is greatly reduced from earlier times. However, in some regions we still have access to a great many sites. University of Maine research in the Boothbay and Muscongus Bay areas of the central Maine coast identified over three hundred extant shell heaps, or shell midden sites. Despite the north-south alignment of the long peninsulas, or necks, the majority of sites do not face only east and west, which they would if they were situated at random. Instead, people had a strong tendency to orient their sites to the south and southeast, and usually in association with a clam-bearing mudflat. The vast majority of shell midden sites were located to take full advantage of water travel, that is, not on exposed rocky areas with high surf, which is hazardous to canoes and people, and not well up into the estuaries where low tide means a long carry over soft mud to water.[20] In short, coastal site locations emphasize these two criteria: proximity to clams and other shellfish, and maximum access to safe and convenient canoe use.

Dave Cook rightly points out that ocean canoeing can be dangerous. For that reason Native people developed long, deep, oceangoing, birchbark canoes capable of handling the marine elements.[21] Smaller craft plied the more protected estuarine regions, crossing the peninsulas through narrow guts or waterways between islands, and were often carried through the routes that Dave Cook refers to as "coastal cutoffs." He cites Pemaquid Point, in the Boothbay region, as a place for small craft to avoid, a view I can endorse based on personal experience. We found archaeological sites around narrow channels, and also at spots known today as carrying places, where a canoe or small boat can be portaged a short distance from one bay into the other. Our analysis of site locations in the Boothbay region indicates that fully thirty-eight percent of sites are reasonably close to either carrying places or inland waterways.[22] Taken in conjunction with other site location characteristics, there can be no doubt about how much water travel dominated the thinking of Maine's coastal Native people.

In pre-European times, when Maine's Native people had full access to their homeland, the birchbark canoe was an indispensable aspect of their culture. We cannot begin to comprehend how they negotiated their homeland without an understanding of how canoes enabled access to interior and coastal landscapes. By combining canoe lore with archaeology, Dave Cook has reminded us of these two inseparable domains.

David Sanger, PhD, Professor Emeritus
Anthropology and Quaternary Studies
Climate Change Institute,
UMaine, Orono

Preface

This book began many years before it was first published in 1985. My fascination with the lore of the Piscataquis/Penobscot region began when I was very young and was stimulated by the Native place names which abound in central Maine where I grew up. One of my first encounters with such a name came as I traveled with my father, Sidney Cook, from our home in Milo to Old Town. We drove through LaGrange over to the Penobscot at Howland and then followed the big river south. Some distance below we approached a bridge in a small village with a sign on the right-hand side of the road with the word, PASSADUMKEAG.

I could not read such a large word and asked Dad what it said. When he said Passadumkeag I laughed and thought it was a fine word and wondered what it meant.

My father did not know except that it was the Penobscot Indian name of the stream and village. Passadumkeag Stream enters their river a few miles above Old Town (whose modern name is a direct translation of *Negas*) and their tribal home on Indian Island. For over 7,000 years human beings have lived there.

Over several decades my interest in the natural and human history of Maine and the Maritime Peninsula was fueled by the new information that geology and archaeology provided. I have learned many and wonderful things. I now know that Passadumkeag means "above the gravel bar," and was an oblique reference to an important canoe route to the eastern regions of Maine and New Brunswick.

Since learning the meaning of this word and many others, I still am drawn to the sounds which evoke the many human generations before us, who knew and loved the land since "time out of mind." This book is my tribute to those anonymous generations who traveled and lived here so long and so well.

To enhance your understanding of the geography of the region and the routes, I encourage you to utilize the following resources: First, and the most easily obtained is *The Maine Atlas and Gazetteer* now in its 25th edition and published by DeLorme of Yarmouth, Maine. If you like topographic maps, go online to the University of

New Hampshire's Historic USGS Maps of New England and NY, in the Digital Collections of the Government Documents Dept. (http://docs.unh.edu/), for free topo downloads or prints. Another internet site which has both topographic maps and satellite photos, also free and downloadable/printable, is Terraserver.com. The Appalachian Mountain Club's River Guide series for the New England States has important information about the routes today and their canoeability. The River Guides can be purchased from: Appalachian Mountain Club, 5 Joy St., Boston, MA 02108.

Valuable assistance was given by the following individuals and institutions. Thanks first to the University of Maine's Fogler Library and Eric Flower, Head of the Special Collections Department. A debt is also owed to the Maine Archaeological Society for support and encouragement. The following MAS members have given their time and assistance: the late Dr. Robson Bonnichsen, Dr. and Mrs. David Sanger, Alice Wellman, Mark Hedden, Dr. Arthur Spiess, and the late Riley Sunderland. Additional thanks to Zip Kellogg, Roger Milliken, Ron Cantner, Helen Dyer, Mike Krepner, and most of all to my wife Meg.

Winthrop, Maine D.S.C.
June, 2006

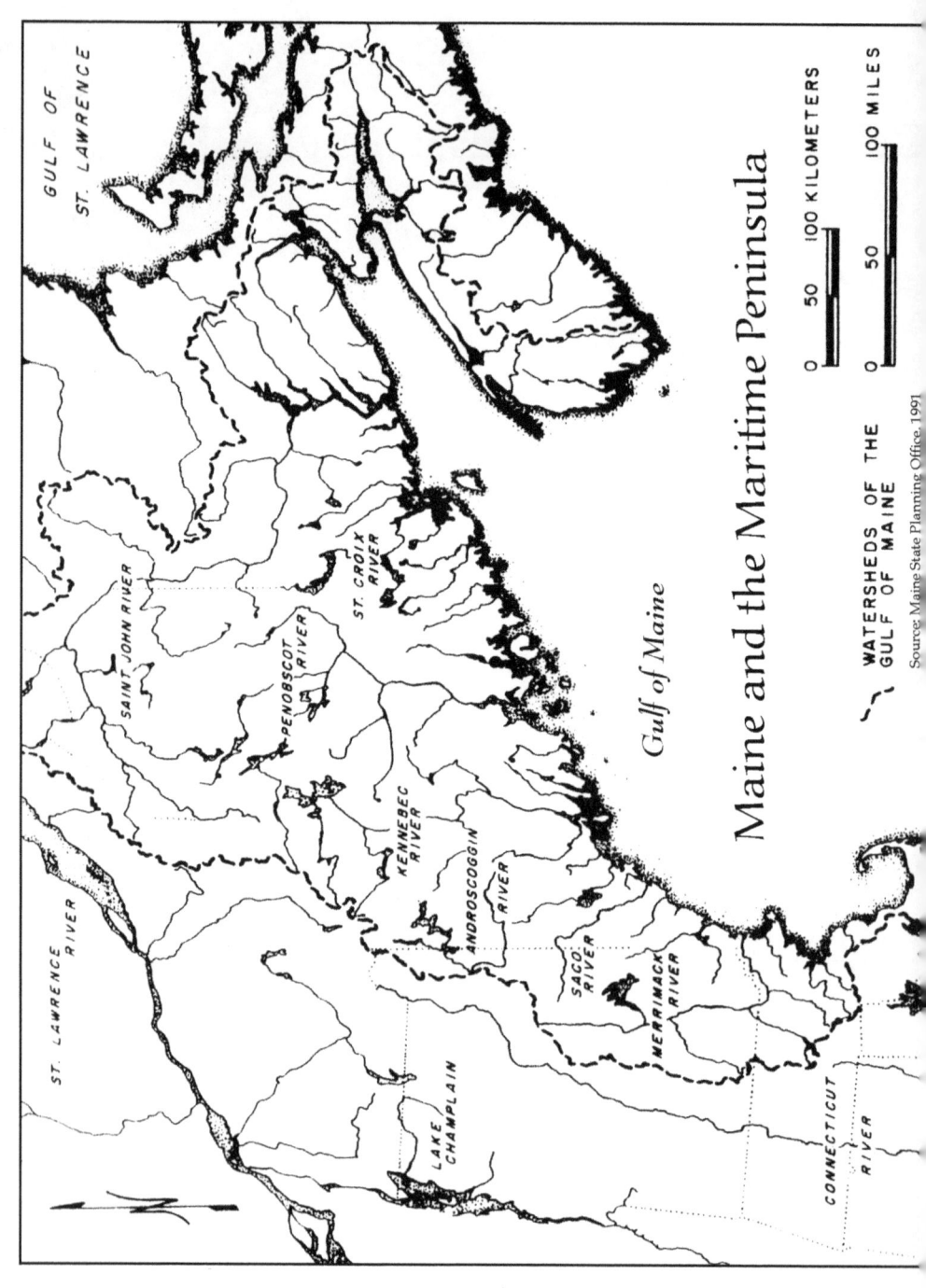

Chapter One

With a Little Help from My Friends

Every spring, summer and fall, thousands of people take to the Maine woods and waters, pursuing the seasonal recreational activities that have made Maine "Vacationland." Cars, trucks, and airplanes speed sportsmen to the most remote corners of Maine in a few hours, but, not too many years ago, places like Caucomgomoc and Munsungan lakes or the West Branch and Allagash River were visited only after a long canoe trip, just as it had been for thousands of years.

Prehistoric people traveled extensively throughout Maine, and when they built the first birchbark canoe, they had the equivalent of the wheel. The birchbark canoe revolutionized the lives of the Native Americans who used them; the multitudinous waterways common to Maine became their highways. Foot travel through the interior of Maine was possible during the ice-free months, but it imposed some severe limitations on the overall behavior of people whose survival depended on their ability to move through very difficult terrain.

The birchbark canoe, whether an invention, innovation, or an idea that was borrowed by the prehistoric Indians of Maine and Canada, liberated its users to travel freely over the thousands of canoe routes that nature so generously provided a wonderful example of man's adaptability to a particular type of environment.

Canoeing today is a sport, but for thousands of years it was a practical necessity. In Maine and much of Canada, canoes are so well suited to the environment we will probably never completely replace them. The only modern improvement made in canoes is the substitution of nearly indestructible space-age materials for fragile birch bark. This has allowed the sport of canoeing to spread much farther than its old natural boundaries, as delineated by the environs of *Betula papyrifera*, the "canoe" or "paper" birch tree. There are probably more canoes in Maine now than at any time in its history, and the growth of the sport attracts new enthusiasts every year. The Maine Department of Environmental Protection, working with the Department of Inland Fisheries and Wildlife (on the issue of invasive aquatic plants) estimated that over 167,000 canoes and kayaks entered the state for the summer of 2001.

Few of the people who travel over the rivers and lakes of Maine realize the important role these waterways and birchbark canoes played in the history of the Native Americans, or of the European soldiers and settlers who fought over and tamed a forest empire. The advantages of canoe travel were so great for the American Indians that canoes and navigable waters became the highways of prehistory.

People who used birchbark canoes conformed their lifeways to that use; canoe travel, like every other form of transportation, imposed limitations which, when combined with an individual's skills, strength, and knowledge, produced, as the anthropologists deem it, "canoe behavior." These limitations are many times less stringent than those imposed on pedestrians in the same land. The canoe made survival tasks much easier for the Indians, and the time saved in food procurement could be invested in other activities not related to survival. The speed and ease of canoe travel, through otherwise forbidding terrain, allowed the Indians to travel long distances to trade, marry, or make war on neighboring tribes and enhanced social and economic activities prohibited to those limited to foot travel or cumbersome dugout canoes. The birchbark canoe was an integral and definitive part of the complex prehistoric cultural organizations that existed in the northeastern forests of Maine, the Maritime Provinces, and westward through Canada. To study the people who lived here for most of Maine's human history and not study the canoe and its use would be like a study of twentieth-century Americans done two thousand years from now that neglects to examine the automobile and its effects on society.

* * *

Before discussing the canoe routes of Maine, I would like to explain how I came to this work and what the major influences are that have shaped it. One factor is the fortuitous dovetailing of my profession, history teacher, and my avocational interests and activities in canoe travel and anthropology/archaeology.

I have been fortunate to have a number of more knowledgeable friends who have helped me along the way. Some of these people are professional anthropologists, like Robson Bonnichsen, David Sanger, and Arthur Spiess, who helped me understand the broad outlines of Maine's prehistory.

Art and I had great fun exploring parts of the Piscataquis Ahwangan many years ago. Rob invited me to Munsungan for a few days back in those heady days after the Paleo-Indian site was discovered in the mid-1970s. Rob had identified an important resource for hunters: "weapons grade" volcanic stone, Munsungan chert (sometimes spelled "Munsungun.") "The chert outcrops on Norway Bluff and Round Mountain drew people like a magnet," Rob said, "and at some point they came by canoe."

Dave Sanger took me under his wing in several ways: First, he was my graduate school advisor and guide through the sometimes choppy waters of an M.A. degree. He also invited me to work on or visit the many sites he investigated in his long career. I'll never forget the day a sea mink skull, a species now extinct, fell out of my pit wall in the clamshell midden I was excavating on Knox Island in Penobscot Bay. I learned a lot from Dave as we paddled along the Aroostook River, visiting known archaeological sites during a "Phase One" investigation prior to the rebuilding of an old dam on the Aroostook River downstream of Ashland. Dave's charge was to write an archaeological impact statement in preparation to organizing a "Phase Two" plan, if the dam was ever carried beyond the planning stage. The dam was never built, and while shoveling out and then refilling many test pits, I also filled in many holes in my understanding of prehistory. One can get education traveling in such company.

But the one who really guided me into this work was, for years, my next-door neighbor who, as a registered guide for over six decades, took hundreds of "sports" into the Maine woods in canoes. My friend and mentor Myron Smart spent over sixty years using canoes as tools. Even well into his eighties, Myron was known as a canoe builder, having made and sold over two hundred after he "retired."

Myron Smart and David Cook ribbing a 15-foot canoe
Photo by Ben Thomas

Smart lived in Milo, Maine, the "town of three rivers," and began his career in the Maine woods in 1915, at the age of fourteen, as a guide on Moose River, Moosehead Lake, and the West Branch of the Penobscot. Such work included arduous poling up Moose River past "Charlie's Corner" and "the Hen and Chickens" toward Brassua, or paddling out onto the lake and heading where the trout were running. Outboard motors were still years in the future, and only the yell of the happy camper or the whoop of a talkative loon broke the big quiet.

Another old-time Moosehead guide, Arthur Johnson of Norridgewock, since deceased and then in his nineties, recounted for me in 1979 his first recollection of Myron. "The first thing I can recall about Myron is seeing him pole an eighteen-foot canoe up Moose River when he was no bigger than that," gesturing out waist high with his hand. "He was just a little boy, but he could already pole a canoe!"[1]

Myron came by his calling naturally and was just one in a long line of Smart men in the Maine woods. In 1779 John Smart, one of Bangor's pioneers, landed near the Penobscot Salmon Pool and hacked a farm and a life out of the forest, establishing the family on the Penobscot.[2] This great river has played a major role in the human history of Maine, and generations of Smarts went upriver and down to hunt, trap, or work in the lumber woods, and the Penobscot was their highway.

Myron's great-grandfather was the famous Captain James L. Smart of Sebec, Maine. "Captain Jim" saw extensive service in the American Civil War, first as a sergeant in the 13th Regiment, Maine Volunteer Infantry, and later as an officer in the Corps de Afrique.[3] His civilian career was in the woods, building dams and bossing woods crews and river drives, including the famous West Branch Drive, the biggest and most important in Maine in the late nineteenth century. Captain Jim, alone or with other well-known river men like John Ross, the "greatest river driver in the world," and Cornelius "Con" Murphy, bossed the West Branch Drive for eleven springs.[4]

When Myron was ten years old, he accompanied his father Frank and grandfather Bill on the Connecticut River Log Drive from

Second Connecticut Lake, on New Hampshire's boundary with Quebec, south to Holyoke, Massachusetts. Frank was boss of the drive that year and had hired his father Bill as his assistant and took Myron along to show him what a big drive was like.

They traveled in a twenty-foot canoe paddled by a Penobscot Indian, Henry Lola. Frank stationed Myron in the front of the canoe and put Henry in charge of him.

His memories of that drive were vivid after nearly seventy-five years and contained more than a little humor. He used to tell this story about his grandfather: When the drive was fairly well along and near the numerous river towns of Vermont and New Hampshire, the head cook came to Frank Smart to complain that bums and hobos were sneaking into the chow line in such numbers that some of the crew there were nearly two hundred men on the drive were not getting their meals. A hungry river driver was potentially a dangerous individual, and Frank was properly concerned. He told Bill, who figured that this was one of those problems that he was hired to handle, and Bill said he would "take care of it."

At the next meal Bill stationed himself aboard the cook's floating kitchen called, on the Connecticut River, the *Mary Ann*. The raft was connected with the shore by two plank walkways: the men went aboard to get their grub on one plank and used the other to get back ashore where they ate.

Hungry men, river drivers and others, lined up on the shore, waiting for the cook to yell, "Come and get it!"

Old Bill "he warn't big but he was tough" stood on the raft eyeing the long line of men.

The average person would have had a very difficult time distinguishing a river driver from a hobo, but Bill had no problem at all. When the first freeloader stepped aboard the *Mary Ann,* Bill knocked him into the Connecticut River. With that, about twenty-five men stepped out of line and headed back to town. "They was pretty rough in those days," Myron noted.

In 1912 Frank Smart took his family to Rockwood, Maine where he had taken a job with the Great Northern Paper Company. Rockwood, on Moosehead Lake, was a major transshipment point for men and equipment going into the Penobscot Woods and "the Northern" had big facilities there to handle those matters. The Smarts lived on the banks of Moose River, and Myron busied himself with school, fishing, and trapping.

Frank Smart died of pneumonia in 1914, and as a result of family needs, Myron took his first job in the winter of 19141915 with the Kellogg Lumber Company then logging the woods of Sandy Bay Township. The camp boss, a friend of his father, had the blacksmith cut a cant dog* down to size for him and put him to work "in the yard."

Logs were hauled by teams from the "chopping" to a place "handy to a good driving chance," where they were piled up in huge roll-ways on the banks of the stream to await the spring drive downriver to the mills at Old Town and Bangor.

Myron worked in this camp for the rest of the winter, and occasionally he drove the "sprinkler" during the nights. The sprinkler was simply a water tank on sled runners that was hauled by a team of horses. During the long winter nights water was sprinkled onto the tote roads to ensure good hauling the next day. Water was obtained from some nearby beaver bog by chopping through the ice and hooking the team up to a device that swung one barrel of water at a time, more or less, into the tank. The team would be reharnessed when the tank was full, and off they would go on their rounds.

Myron volunteered to drive the sprinkler, and, since he was somewhat independent, he hooked up the team and left camp before anybody could give him any advice. After all, he could handle a team with no problem, he thought.

He drove the outfit out onto the ice of a nearby beaver flowage and filled the tank up to the brim. He started off on his rounds, thinking that he was very efficient because he had filled the tank up so full. He was not bothered by the fact that there was no hatch cover for the tank.

---

*Otherwise known as a "Peavey," named after Joseph Peavey of Stillwater, Maine, who improved on the cant dog, this is a tool with a sharp spike, used for handling logs.

After a short way, he came to a steep hill which he had to descend, and, as the sprinkler had no brakes, he would need to be "snubbed down." There was a small camp on the hill, and a "snub man" stayed there all the time when there was any sledding to do. He hooked the logging sleds up to his snubber* and played out his rope a little at a time. Losing control on a steep hill, the teamsters called it "getting sluiced," was almost certain death to the teamster and his horses.

Myron hooked up to the snubber, and he had the horses pull the sprinkler forward. The tub was full, sloshing over the top, and there was a little slack in the rope, so the sled ran forward about ten feet. The rope then snubbed up, bringing the sled to an abrupt halt on the steep slope and launching a tidal wave of cold, beaver-bog water over Myron who was standing on the whiffletree driving the team.

He then realized that he had overfilled the tank for the rough terrain, and he also realized he had to finish his tour of duty soaking wet. He was well togged in wool, but, as it was January and about twenty-five degrees below zero, he did get cold. "I got done about two o'clock in the morning and could hardly move. I was cold and my clothes had frozen. I walked stiff legged unhitching the team, and my pants stood up by themselves."

He went to bed leaving the frozen wool pants standing in front of the woodstove. When the first of the crew saw them, they knew the quiet young boy had gotten splashed, and they were grinning when Myron woke up.

After that winter's work was done, Myron worked as a guide on Moose River. His routine would begin when he picked up a "sport" at one of the then numerous riverside hotels. They would head up the Moose to fish the pools between "the Lake" (as Moosehead is known in that neck of the woods) and Brassua Lake. He also paddled his sports out onto Moosehead to fish the inlets and deep holes for the big togue.

During his first guiding summer, Myron hired out as the junior member of a five-guide team that took four sports from Moosehead

---

*A machine that used friction to lower heavily loaded sleds down steep hills.

1. With a Little Help from My Friends

down the St. John in canoes. Myron was the "chore boy" around the camp and handled the "wangan" canoe. The other guides had some of the gear and a sport in their canoes, but Myron was alone in a twenty-footer with the "wangan." In Maine and throughout canoe country, that old Indian word* refers to all the impedimenta of canoe travel; the food, tents, etc., and it was up to him to paddle and pole the loaded canoe wherever they went. For this work he received $2.00 per day, standard wages for that time.

One of the guides, one of the "Henderson boys from Caucomgomoc," tried to frighten the rookie guide with tales about the dangers of the St. John. But Roy Nicholas, an old Penobscot Indian guide and the head cook on this trip, took the boy under his wing and told him to "do what I do and you will make it better than him."

Nicholas had some fifty guiding summers behind him and knew every brook, stream, bog, or swamp where "a man could push a canoe." He was well known for his woods craft and he taught Myron many of the tricks of the guiding profession.

Myron had wanted to be a guide, even as a young boy, because he had noticed that the guides always looked like they were having a good time. He eventually found out that guiding was not an easy job and that it wasn't fun all of the time. He once told his father he wanted to be a guide, and Frank didn't know why anyone would want to be a "damned skunk hunter," but Myron did.

Myron absorbed much of his knowledge about the woods and woods' ways from guides like Roy Nicholas, and he fondly recalled many of these men whom he first met when he was very young

---

*Wangan, also seen as "wanigan," or in place names as "ahwangan," refers to the gear that one would carry in the canoe. My old friend Myron always referred to his wangan when talking about such. It also means "a carry" when incorporated in a name. Wangan Brook drains the same swamp as the brook at the head of Joe Merry Lake on the West Branch Penobscot, and the name indicates a connection between tributaries of the Penobscot. The Pleasant River, a branch of the Piscataquis, rises just south of and intermingles with the West Branch Penobscot drainage, and for canoeists this was a direct connection to the interior of the state. This general set of routes was referred to as the "Piscataquis Ahwangan" and contains a lot of archaeology beginning around ten thousand years ago.

and they were very old. He also found time to finish high school and then attend the Bangor School of Commerce where he learned "clerking."

Besides being a fishing and hunting guide, Myron also trapped and worked on the Moose River drive for several springs as canoeman for the boss of the drive. He was skilled with all the tools of the river driver's trade, the axe, pick pole, and Peavey, but he was just as skilled in handling a canoe, and keeping a set of books and tally sheets. Since these skills were in short supply on Moose River, Myron seldom got his feet wet, or at least very wet, and he has noted with satisfaction that "a pencil is a damnsight easier to handle than a Peavey, and it paid better."

At the beginning of World War II, after thirty years of this kind of life and with a wife and four children, Myron became a game warden for the state of Maine, and later he served as a biologist for the Game Division of the Department of Inland Fisheries and Wildlife that was back when everyone called it simply, "Fish and Game." In all of his work, canoes were important tools that made him more efficient. His clear and cogent recollections have helped guide me into this work, because he gave me a practical understanding of canoes and the ways they have been used for thousands of years. This understanding has helped me appreciate Fannie Hardy Eckstorm, the other major influence on this work.

In 1978 I obtained Jeanne Patten Whitten's excellent bibliography of the voluminous Eckstorm papers which are stored in Fogler Library at the University of Maine, Orono.[5] I noticed several references to unpublished material about prehistoric Indian canoe routes which were of great interest to me, and, I hope, to others. Those notes form the core of this work.

Fannie Hardy was born June 18, 1865, into a distinguished Maine family. Her grandfather was a fur trader in the Penobscot region, and her uncle, Jeremiah P. Hardy, was famous as a portraitist. Manly Hardy, her father, was also a successful fur trader and self-taught ornithologist, and he loved the woods and waters of Maine. He passed this love on to his daughter, and for this Maine is beholden to Manly Hardy.[6]

As a child Fannie Hardy had many Indian playmates and neighbors in Brewer. She often accompanied her father on fur-buying trips to Old Town where she became widely known and liked by the tribe. She was a close observer of the Penobscot from her childhood and was a student of their language.

Educated at a public school in Brewer, Miss Hardy attended Abbott Academy in Andover, Massachusetts, and later graduated from Smith College in 1888.[7]

That summer, for a graduation present, she accompanied her father on a canoe trip down the East Branch of the Penobscot and the following summer they canoed down the West Branch where she saw firsthand the setting of much of her future work.

In 1893 Fannie married Jacob A. Eckstorm, an Episcopal priest from Chicago. The Eckstorms lived in Oregon for one year before they moved back to Rhode Island where, in 1899, the Reverend Eckstorm died, leaving his wife with two small children: a son, Paul, and a daughter, Katherine, who died at age seven. Mrs. Eckstorm returned home to Brewer to live in a house her father owned on Wilson Street and for the next forty-seven years immersed herself in the life and legend of Maine as few have done.[8]

Mrs. Eckstorm began serious research into her several areas of interest while still in college. Over the long years of her life, she produced over two hundred published pieces on natural and human history, language, folklore, and minstrelsy. She was a recognized authority on ornithology and was invited to join the prestigious American Ornithologists' Union while still in college.[9] In fact, she was the author of several standard books on United States birds; *The Woodpecker* (Boston, 1904) is an example.

The topic of Indian canoe routes first appears in her notes entitled *Indian Trails of Maine*, a paper she read before the Nineteenth Century Club of Bangor, October 29, 1920. In 1929 she delivered essentially the same paper in Brewer to another historical group. The talk was covered by a local newspaper, and an article followed which, in customary Fannie Hardy Eckstorm fashion, she deplored because the article was garbled.

In 1929 she wrote a letter to her friend and colleague, Dr. William

Francis Ganong, the noted New Brunswick historian and former professor at Smith, stating that she was going to write a paper on the topic of canoe routes for the Maine State Library.[10] Mrs. Eckstorm never finished this work; the Great Depression probably wiped out the money that would have been used in publication.

One of her chief objectives was to preserve for future researchers information about Indian life and culture at a time when it was fast disappearing. The strengths and weaknesses of Mrs. Eckstorm's work on Indian canoe routes seem fully apparent to me. Her information about the Penobscot watershed is far more complete than it is for neighboring systems. This was her area of expertise, and her notes show that she never finished researching the topic, as some were made after the initial draft was done in 1929.

I have expanded the scope of the material by drawing on my own experience and research as well as the work of others.

Mrs. Eckstorm's knowledge of the Indian place names of Maine is very valuable: "These old names are the colored curtains which hung beside the windows through which we look back into the beginnings of human living here; for ages and ages, countless human beings have lived and toiled and suffered here, and have left only these names."[11]

When properly understood, many of the old Indian names, relics in their own right, add another clue about life in ancient times. Maine has many Indian names extant, but many are misapplied. Native Americans named specific spots according to their most outstanding characteristic. Names like Saco, "a stream of water" (running into the ocean), Kennebec, "the long reach," or Androscoggin, "place for curing fish," are names of specific places which are now incorrectly the names of large rivers, lakes, streams, and mountains. Most of the place names have an *upstream* perspective; that is, they are best understood if you remember that the Indians chose them when traveling upstream in birchbark canoes.

As Mrs. Eckstorm has noted, "the little rivers named themselves." If the stream was an important fishing spot, the name would reflect that importance. Cobbossee, "where they spear sturgeon by torchlight," and Madamiscontis, "plenty of alewives," are two of many examples. If an important canoe route lay along a certain waterway, that might be a feature in the name: Sebasticook, "the short route," or the more exotic sounding Oodoolseezicook-Ahwangan, "the Entrails Pond route," are examples.

Many of the place names contain indications of the canoeing difficulties found along a river or stream. In the Penobscot watershed, names abound with the suffix *ticook*, or its variations, and it is associated with a deadwater. Chimskiticook, "big deadwater," or Skiticook, "a deadwater," are examples. The term "deadwater" does not mean dead in the sense of no current, but dead in the sense that there are no difficult portages or dangerous places.

Another suffix, also frequently found in Penobscot country, is found in words like Nesowadnehunk, which means "stream that runs between the mountains" an apt name, as anyone who knows that stream can agree Sededunkehunk, "rapids at the mouth," Madunkehunk, "height of land stream," and always describes a difficult place for canoeists. The *hunk* sound in these words hints at the grunting of one on a portage or of one shoving a canoe upstream "on the pole." No Penobscot canoeman would ever mistake a *ticook* stream for a *hunk* stream, and these names were telltale guides for a mapless people.

While some of the old names are misapplied, others are still as good as ever and sometimes should be heeded. A friend of mine had an experience that illustrates this nicely. Several years ago he decided to retrace part of the old Chaudière/Penobscot/Kennebec canoe route by flying into Penobscot Lake on the Maine-Quebec border and canoeing down from there to the West Branch, Penobscot, and then to Moosehead Lake via Northwest Carry. Penobscot Lake, remote and beautiful, was once part of one of the most important canoe routes connecting Maine with the mighty St. Lawrence, and my friend thought the upper section would be good canoeing.

The Indian name for the small brook out of Penobscot Lake is O'zwazo-ge-hunk, "when they come by here they wade their canoes," and it hints at two things: low water and, in the *hunk* part of the name, a real hard go for some of the way.[12] I knew this old name but my friend didn't and, upon his return, I was eager to hear his account. "The trip was OK, except for the first six miles down Penobscot Brook," he told me. "The water was too low for us and the canoes, so we waded them where we could and carried them where we had to, until we got down to deeper channels where the stream flattens out a little." When I told him what O'zwazo-ge-hunk meant he heartily concurred with its modern applicability and said he wished he had known it before he left, and he vowed to study the Indian place names with more than a casual interest in the future.

Mrs. Eckstorm died in 1946 as a respected authority in her fields of endeavor. The scope of her work is impressive and spans the ages from the prehistoric to the end of the logging era in Maine in the early twentieth century. In recognition of her contributions she received an honorary Master of Arts Degree from the University of Maine in 1920. In 1946, after her death, she was made an Honorary Member of the New Brunswick Museum, the first woman so distinguished.

I hope that she would be pleased by my effort to bring this topic to light, but I have trepidations as I know her attitude about such efforts that fall short of the mark.

My goal is to define the limits of canoe use in Maine by outlining the routes and discussing the seasonal variables that affect canoe travel, while providing a brief historical and geological background.

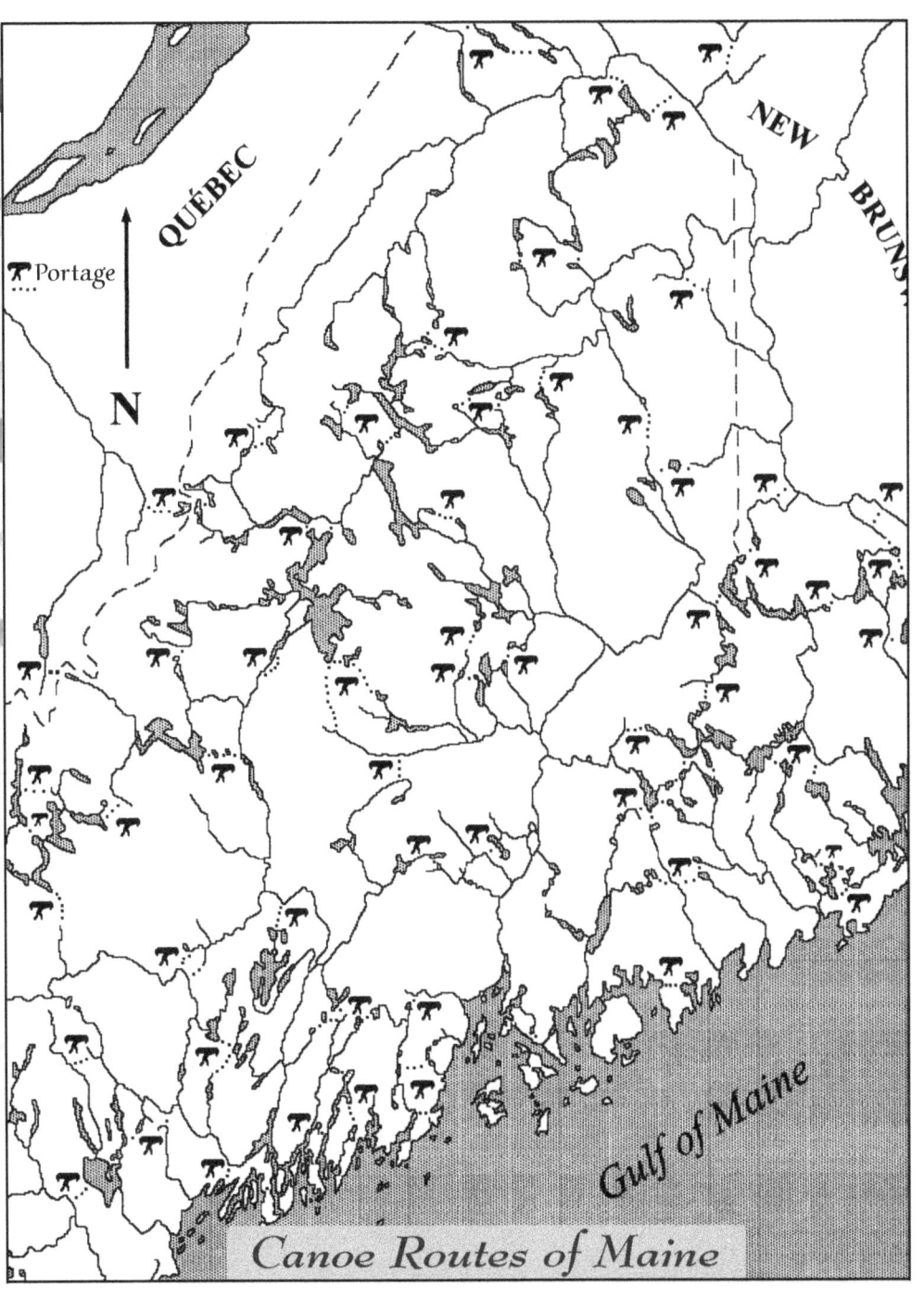

Chapter Two

Land and Water

Maine and much of Canada are covered with thick forests and an incredible number of freshwater lakes, rivers, and streams. In Maine's 33,000 square miles there are over 6,000 lakes and ponds drained by 32,000 miles of rivers, brooks, and streams.[1]

The modern forests and river systems have not always existed here. When the first people, Paleo-Indians, penetrated into the interior 12,000 years ago, they faced an environment that would be strange and forbidding to us. These people came into Maine on the heels of the retreating glacier and, anthropologists hypothesize, large herds of caribou or other types of animals that grazed on the herbs, sedge, grass, and mosses that grew here. A sheet of ice evidently remained astride northern Maine for some time, an island of ice that would affect local weather patterns and, as it slowly settled and melted, created many lakes and rivers which drained south.[2]

By 10,000 years ago forests composed of spruce, fir, red pine, poplar, and birch began to appear; most probably these first forests were surrounded by large grasslands.

As time passed and the environment changed, new species, such as oak and white pine, gained footholds and became established. Hardwoods dominated the period from 8,000 to 4,800 years ago. Spruce and fir decreased while white pine, birch, ash, maple, hemlock, and after 5,000 years ago, beech, proliferated.[3]

Such vegetational changes suggest climatic changes. The human population was presented with a new set of challenges and, at the same time, presented with new opportunities created by ecological flux.

2. Land and Water

About 12,000 years ago, when the Atlantic Ocean was several hundred feet higher and the Penobscot and Kennebec valleys were large bays, Paleo-Indians found and had begun to exploit an outcropping of hardened volcanic ooze called "chert" on Norway Bluff and at Round Mountain in northern Maine.[4] We assume that these people came on foot and that they did not have boats of any kind, either of bark or skin.

Foot travelers could have walked over much of interior Maine on glacial gravel deposits known as "eskers" and "kames" and called "horsebacks." There are many such deposits that seem to wander for miles across the bogs and wetlands of Maine, and they have been used for modern roadbeds. Being gravel, they are firm and well drained but tend to be crooked and rollercoaster-like.* A number of these horsebacks have been traced one hundred miles and a few stretch more than one hundred and fifty. In general, they run from the northwest to the southeast, accompanying the rivers, sometimes on one side, sometimes on the other. They have even been found on both sides of some rivers.

Eskers and kames are not limited to the modern rivers and often are seen running off through the country as high gravel ridges; these may have been the first highways for aboriginal hunters.

The melting of the massive ice cap, maybe two miles thick, relieved the earth of its tremendous weight. Slowly the flat terrain of the tundra began to crumple upward creating hills and valleys. Geologists call this "isostatic rebound." So along with the changing temperature and the concurrent changes in plant and animal life, the face of the earth actually changed too.

By 5,000 years ago the river systems of Maine assumed their present locations, but this does not mean that channels have not migrated back and forth in their broad and flat valleys; rivers are dynamic and so were the people who came to live along their banks.

The modern river systems of Maine, New Brunswick, and southern Quebec all rise and flow from the same general highland,

---

*Ask anyone who has traveled Route 9 between Bangor and Calais about the road.

their headwaters practically intermingled. From this central plateau, in northwestern Maine and neighboring Quebec, the St. John, Penobscot, Kennebec, Androscoggin, Chaudière, and Connecticut rivers began their runs to the sea in all directions. As they flow down they are enlarged by thousands of tributaries some are large rivers in their own right that flow perpendicular to the main river from regions where their headwaters also intermingle with adjacent watersheds.

The birchbark canoe represents the best adaptation that the people made during their long residence in the northern forests, but this option was not open to the Indians in southern New England.

The land west of the Saco River was not so well suited for a canoe adaptation as the eastern and northern regions, but it was easier for foot travelers. The terrain is much drier and lacks the thick forests of Maine and Quebec. A wide sandy plateau of glacial wash from higher lands extends most of the way to the Connecticut River, a level plain covered with pitch pine, *Pinus rigida*.

During the Indian Wars, this region was frequently traversed by large scouting parties of colonial soldiers who marched where they pleased and used prominent hills as navigational aids. Marc Lescarbot, the French historian, noted that beyond the Saco "the Indians have made little paths from place to place, which is not the case at Port Royal Annapolis, Nova Scotia, and their forests are not thick, and moreover much of the land is open."[5] Lescarbot was speaking specifically about Cape Cod, but the description is appropriate for the country west of the Piscataqua River.

Southern New England had many lakes and ponds, as well as many brooks and streams. But compared to Maine and Canada, it was insufficiently watered for canoe routes and lacked birch bark for canoes; instead, large and heavy dugout canoes were used. These craft are best used along the deep and gentle sections of a river and were used to good advantage. Dugouts are heavy and tended to soak up water, becoming heavier. They could not be portaged great distances around waterfalls or between watersheds like the birchbark canoes to the north. These peripheral tribes may have obtained birchbark canoes by means of trade and used them in conjunction with dugouts.

As a result, the Indians of lower New England had many paths, some so well known that they are mentioned in colonial records.

The old Bay Path from Massachusetts Bay to the Connecticut River was the most famous, and as soon as the English introduced horses, it became a road. The Pequot Path, from Providence to Westerly, Rhode Island; the Nipmuck Path, from near Norwich, Connecticut, to Eastford; the Mohawk Trail, from the Deerfield Valley to North Adams, Massachusetts, and several paths clearly marked on early maps of Vermont were all well known to the Native Americans.

During the so-called Indian Wars many English captives were taken over such paths to Canada, and some had their experiences recorded verifying the existence of the trails.

There were few paths of note in prehistoric Maine. One was the Saco Path; one branch went from near Fryeburg up through Crawford Notch into the White Mountains; the other went south to Lake Winnipesaukee. Professor David C. Smith told me that a well-marked Indian trail was visible along the banks of the Little Androscoggin in the 1930s and 1940s.

Conditions in Maine, therefore, were different from those in the other New England states where fixed trails were a necessity. There may have been many local paths, not counting portage routes, and probably some long overland routes in Maine, but they have left little trace in the records.

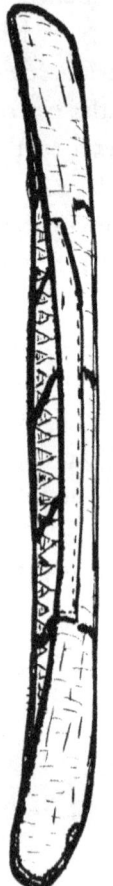
Micmac 14' 2" Pack Canoe

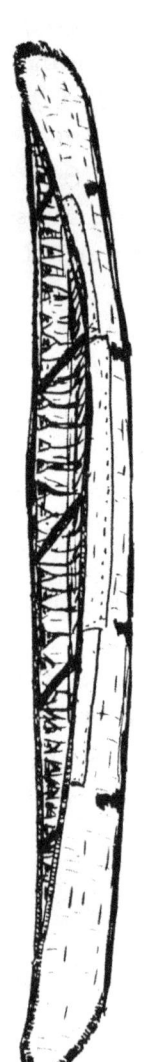
Micmac 17' 4"

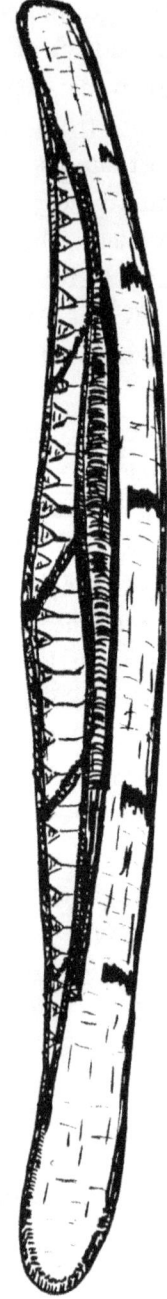
Micmac 21' 8" Ocean Canoe

Illustration by author, after E. T. Adney, and H. I. Chapelle, *Bark Canoes and Skin Boats of North America*

Chapter Three

The Canoes

The birchbark canoe "was the most complex and intricate product of Native mechanical genius in the North."[1] Birchbark canoes are of ancient origin, but we cannot give a definitive date for their first use or properly give credit to the people who invented them.

The birchbark canoe may have been invented locally, or it may have been adopted from some other group.

Siberian tribes, the Yakuts, Tungus, Khants, Mansi, Evenks, Nanays, Udegeys, and Orochi all used birchbark boats to paddle, pole, and portage their way up and down stream.[2]

Edwin Tappan Adney, the best authority on birchbark canoes, thought that some people came from Siberia in such craft, but this view is not held by many modern anthropologists. We do know that the birchbark canoe could not have existed in Maine in the days of the Paleo-Indian. They lived in an Arctic environment devoid of the necessary wood and bark. If they had any boats at all, they would have been skin kayaks, or umiaks, familiar in the Arctic regions since prehistoric times.

As the ice melted, ocean levels rose, dramatically inundating places in southern and central Maine. Millinocket on the Penobscot and Bingham on the Kennebec were very near to great salt bays. During this time Paleo-Indian sites that may have existed along the coast of Maine were flooded and remain so today.

By 9,000 years ago, lowered ocean levels and the crumpling effect of isostatic rebound had, along with warmer weather, created an environment in which birchbark canoes *could have* been made and used. All of the raw materials, birch bark for the covering, black spruce for lashings and pitch, and cedar trees, were here along with human beings who had to travel through the generally rough and swampy land.

If the Paleo-Indians did have skin boats, they became obsolete as a result of the changing environment. The raw materials disappeared, and the water travel conditions changed from large salt bays and huge glacial lakes to rapidly flowing rivers connecting the lakes. Skin craft are well suited for use on big lakes or bays but are easily damaged by rocks so common on shallow rivers.

Dugout canoes, an important invention in their own right, were a later development. Trees big enough for such boats do not exist in a tundra environment. Dugouts were not unknown in Maine and were also used along the lower St. John and St. Lawrence. But, this was at the same time that birchbark canoes were in common use and dugouts were probably an alternative to birchbark canoes along the deep estuaries or on the many lakes.

Florida scientists have been studying the importance of the dugout canoe to prehistoric people there. One hundred and fifteen dugouts have been recovered after being submerged in lakes and swamps for centuries. These slender craft range from fifteen feet up to forty-six feet in length. This study has some direct implications for Maine prehistory, even if the early Mainers never used dugouts.

The dugout, bullboat, and bark canoes are all adaptive mechanisms that helped ease the burdens of human survival. Water travel provided the prehistoric Floridians, low energy users normally, with a high energy source. The Florida research has shown that when four people traveled fifty miles by dugout, they collectively saved 25,000 calories enough to sustain the band for an entire day. "In effect water transportation functioned as a means of building 'capital', and the time and energy saved were applied to activities not directly related to subsistence."[3]

Certainly the same can be said of the importance of water travel in Maine. Compared to Florida's flat landscape, Maine is very rough. The placid waters of the Everglades are mild when compared to the tumultuous waterways that characterize the inland rivers of the Pine Tree State. Foot travel in Maine requires a great deal of energy.

3. The Canoes

From my own experience afoot and in canoes, I would argue that the energy savings are even greater when traveling by birchbark canoe through Maine. The birchbark canoe is much lighter and was used in a more versatile manner than possible with dugouts. The birchbark canoe can easily be propelled upstream through all but the most difficult rapids, even when loaded with several hundred pounds of wangan. To move the same amount of weight on foot would be impossible.

It is often pointed out by those who denigrate the cultural achievements of the Native American that "they never even invented the wheel." In Maine, and in much of North America, there was a very good reason for that: The wheel had absolutely no application in a region of unbroken forests. The people of the Maine and Canadian woods didn't need the wheel, for they had something far better; they had the birchbark canoe.

The Penobscot tribe called their creation *agwiden*, which means "floats lightly,"[4] and they were on the move constantly and often covered great distances. The travels of Penobscot chief Loron during the summer of 1750 are an extreme example. In one summer Loron traveled from Penobscot to Boston by canoe, and back.

He then set out for Quebec via the Piscataquis Ahwangan to Moosehead Lake and North Branch Penobscot Chaudière route. From Quebec he returned to Old Town by the same route and once there rested but briefly before paddling back to Boston. Now that is a paddling journey of significant distance.

A statement made in 1793 by Colonel John Allan testifies to the mobility of canoe people:

> The very easy conveyance by the lakes, rivers and streams so interspersed in this country, they can easy take their women, children, and baggage, where ever their interest, curiosity, or caprice may lead them, and their natural propensity for roving is such that you will see families in the course of a year go through the greatest part of this extent.[5]

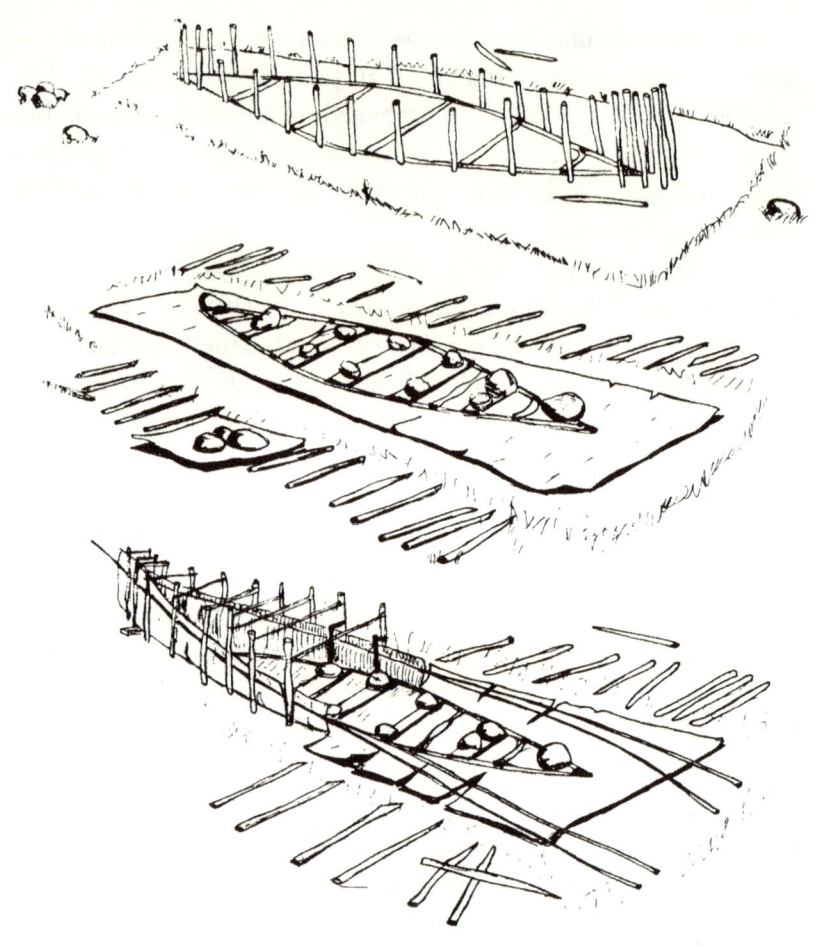

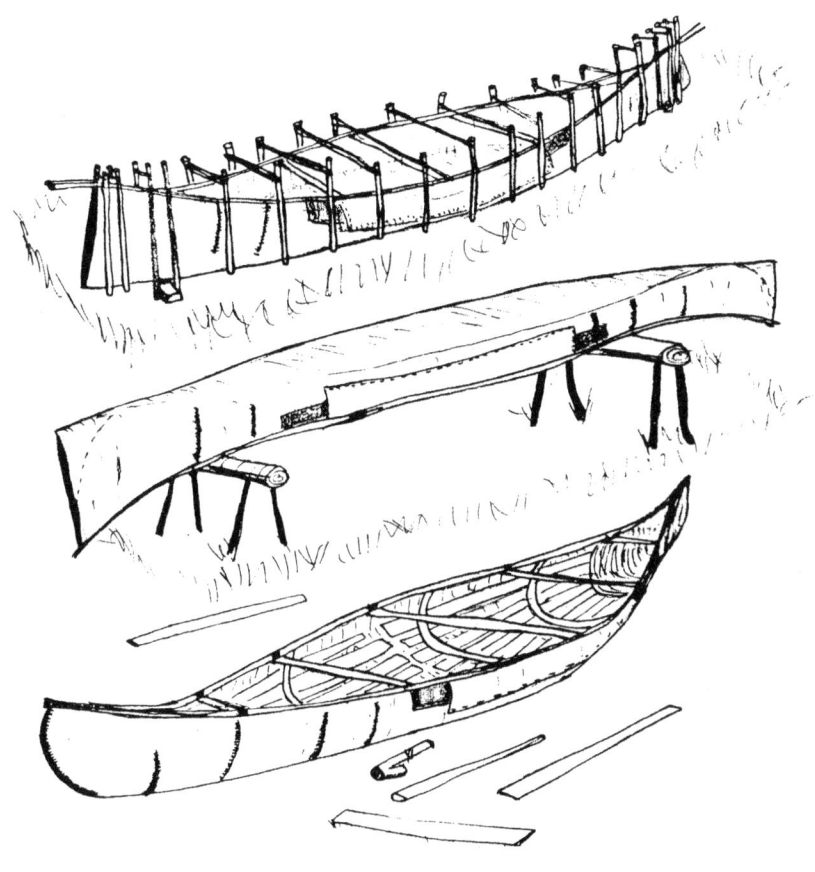

Illustrations by author, after E. T. Adney, and H. I. Chapelle, *Bark Canoes and Skin Boats of North America*

Their trade was important to them even though they did not have agriculture or manufacturing beyond their needs. The volume carried might not be great, but relative to their needs, the necessity for intercommunication between places lying as far apart as Albany, Boston, Montreal, Quebec, the Bay of Chaleur, Nepisiquit, and Chignectou was often imperative, and they had to know the speediest way of sending messengers, if not goods, from place to place.

The canoe was a departure from the small boats of the European explorers. Unlike the rowed longboats, the bark canoe was propelled by a single bladed paddle or setting pole with the voyager facing the direction of travel, a necessity when navigating on shallow and swift streams.[6]

Early European explorers were impressed with the amount of cargo bark canoes could hold and the speed with which they could be paddled. Jacques Cartier recorded the first-known reference to birchbark canoes at the Bay of Chaleur and Prince Edward Island in 1535.[7] He also recorded the fact, as did Captain John Smith to the south years later, that the Native canoes could be paddled much faster than fully manned English longboats could be rowed.

The quality of workmanship of the canoes also drew favorable comments. In 1603 James Rosier noted that

> their canoes are made without any iron, of bark of the birch tree, strengthened within the ribs and hoops of wood in so good fashion, with such excellent ingenious art, as they are able to beare seven or eight persons far exceeding any seen in the Indies.[8]

There were three types of canoes in the Northeast when the first Europeans began taking note of such things.

Tribal variations were not only expressions of taste but also adaptations of a general concept to specific needs. Modern canoes generally conform to the ancient specifications and reveal ancient advantages and disadvantages when they are used.

The largest canoes were the ocean canoes, eighteen to twenty-two feet long. They were used in the dangerous waters of coastal Maine and Canada where large waves and stiff winds are common. In 1535 Jacques Cartier reported seeing two bark canoes containing a total of seventeen people. Undoubtedly he saw ocean canoes. In such canoes the Indians hunted and fished along the coast with numerous shortcut portages across the peninsulas and islands.

River canoes were sixteen to eighteen feet in length and had a rounded hull when compared to their oceangoing cousins. Round bottomed canoes are much more responsive in quick water than flatter versions.

The smallest type of canoe was the "woods" or "pack" canoe. These were eleven to fourteen feet long and made to be portaged by hunters and trappers as they scoured remote bogs and swamps for their prey. They were very light and easy to paddle but were so small that they were of little use in shallow water (a twelve-foot canoe requires more water to float than an eighteen footer) or on exposed lakes and bays.

The different canoes were all made in the same manner and of the same materials. The outside covering was of thick birch bark turned inside out and fitted with a lengthwise lining of thin strips of white cedar.

The hulls were stiffened and shaped by shaved cedar ribs which were held in place by lashing them with spruce root to long cedar rails. Five hardened thwarts, carved from birch or maple for strength, were fitted and lashed into the rails as well.

The rails went the whole length of the canoe and were joined at the bow and stern by wooden pegs and lashed with spruce roots. The ends of Maine canoes were fairly flat, never rounded backwards, and they made a streamlined silhouette from stem to stern.

The weight of a canoe varies with its length, width, thickness of the bark, and the dryness of the canoe. It is interesting to note that there is a general weight-to-strength ratio that, until the development of the lightweight plastics of the last twenty years, established equivalent weights for canoes no matter what they were made from. An eighteen-foot canoe of birch bark, wood/canvas, aluminum or fiberglass weighs about eighty-five pounds; a fifteen-foot canoe weighs about sixty pounds and so on.

Photo Margaret Cook

The birch bark was fitted by seams, sewed with split spruce roots and made watertight by "pitching" the seams with a boiled mixture of spruce resin, charcoal, and fat. Nicholas Denys, published in 1672, says that in the very early times spruce gum was used after it had been chewed, making it soft. In a good canoe there never was a seam across the bottom until some accident made one necessary. Then the bark from a small tree was sewed in and liberally pitched.

For inland use, the full equipment of a canoe was two long rock maple paddles *tohque' ngau* to the Penobscots and an eight- to ten-foot long ash setting pole, which they called *gikque' mkwahque* and means "prods under the water," an apt description.[9] Indians also often had a "headboard" whittled from a piece of cedar and loosely tied to the center thwart. They also rigged a cedar bark tumpline from the ends of the center thwart across their foreheads. When they were carrying the canoes the headboard and tumpline evenly distributed the weight and balanced the canoe, greatly easing the task (further discussion in Chapter 4).

Equipment for ocean canoeing included paddles, but instead of a setting pole the Indians carried a long spear to recover the bodies of seals and porpoises. They also carried an anchor with line and a birchbark container of fresh water. After the Europeans arrived the Passamaquoddies became bold sailors by attaching a small spritsail to their seaworthy canoes.

The Indians also made temporary canoes out of other barks and out of moose hides. Not as good as birchbark canoes, these craft were for limited duty, such as crossing a lake, or making a quick run downriver.

The Iroquois, for example, made canoes of elm and oak bark and La Hontan reported in 1703 that some could carry up to thirty men. He said

> the canoes the Iroquois provide themselves with are so unwieldy and large that they do not approach the speed of those made of birch bark. They are made of elm bark, which is naturally heavy and the shape they give them is awkward; they are so long and so broad that thirty men can row in them, two-by-two, seated or standing, fifteen to each rank, but the freeboard is so low that when any little wind arises they are sensible enough not to navigate the lakes.

Moosehide canoes, called "bullboats" were built by the Micmacs and Maliseets for use in traveling downriver from their winter hunting grounds to where they had hidden their birchbark canoes the previous fall. Green moose hides were shaved to remove the hair then sewed over a crude frame and covered with spruce pitch for waterproofing. When they had finished with the bullboats, they were taken apart and the hides tanned and used to make moccasins.

Rafts of logs were also quickly made by Indians to cross still bodies of water.

A single log could be used to cross a stream if necessary. A certain old-time guide would occasionally cross the Penobscot by taking a crooked cedar log from his rail fence and, with a long pole, he would push or splash his way across the Penobscot River, even though the log sank more than a foot under water. This could not have been done by the early Natives, because it took the training of the river driver to perform such a feat of balancing, and dry logs were usually unobtainable in the forest.

One of the most important qualities of the canoe was, and still is, the ability to be poled upstream. The paddle can be used when the water is deep and not too swift, but there are hundreds of rapid streams, too shallow for paddling, that were important Indian canoe routes. Even heavily laden canoes are easily propelled with a setting pole up most streams, and an experienced hand can go against a swift current with surprising ease and speed.

My experience in *upstream* canoe travel on Maine rivers indicates that two miles per hour is an average speed with a loaded canoe carries excluded.

The seventeenth-century English and French admired the workmanship and handling qualities of the birchbark canoes and found them to be indispensable in their exploring and military activities. Samuel de Champlain was the first European to use canoes in his exploration of the Canadian interior; he almost drowned on the St. Lawrence when he and his Indian guides swamped their canoes in Lachine Rapids near Montreal. He was seeking the mythical Northwest Passage through North America to the Pacific and Asia, and Champlain himself named these rapids *La Chine* or "China" Rapids, after his belief that he had finally discovered the elusive route to the Orient.

The explorations on the St. Lawrence and Mississippi by Jacques Marquette and Louis Jolliet are well known, and they traveled in canoes.

Later the English took to canoes as well because, like the French, they realized that only the network of canoe routes made rapid travel through the forests possible.

The significance of Quebec to the history of New England may not be obvious, but it underlies all of our early colonial history. Quebec is the key to all the water communication north and south.

As mentioned earlier, all of the large rivers of the Gulf of Maine rise in a range of highlands far from their mouths. Their headwaters are nearly intermingled and lie comparatively near the St. Lawrence and run in all directions. The St. Lawrence tributaries, the St. Francis,

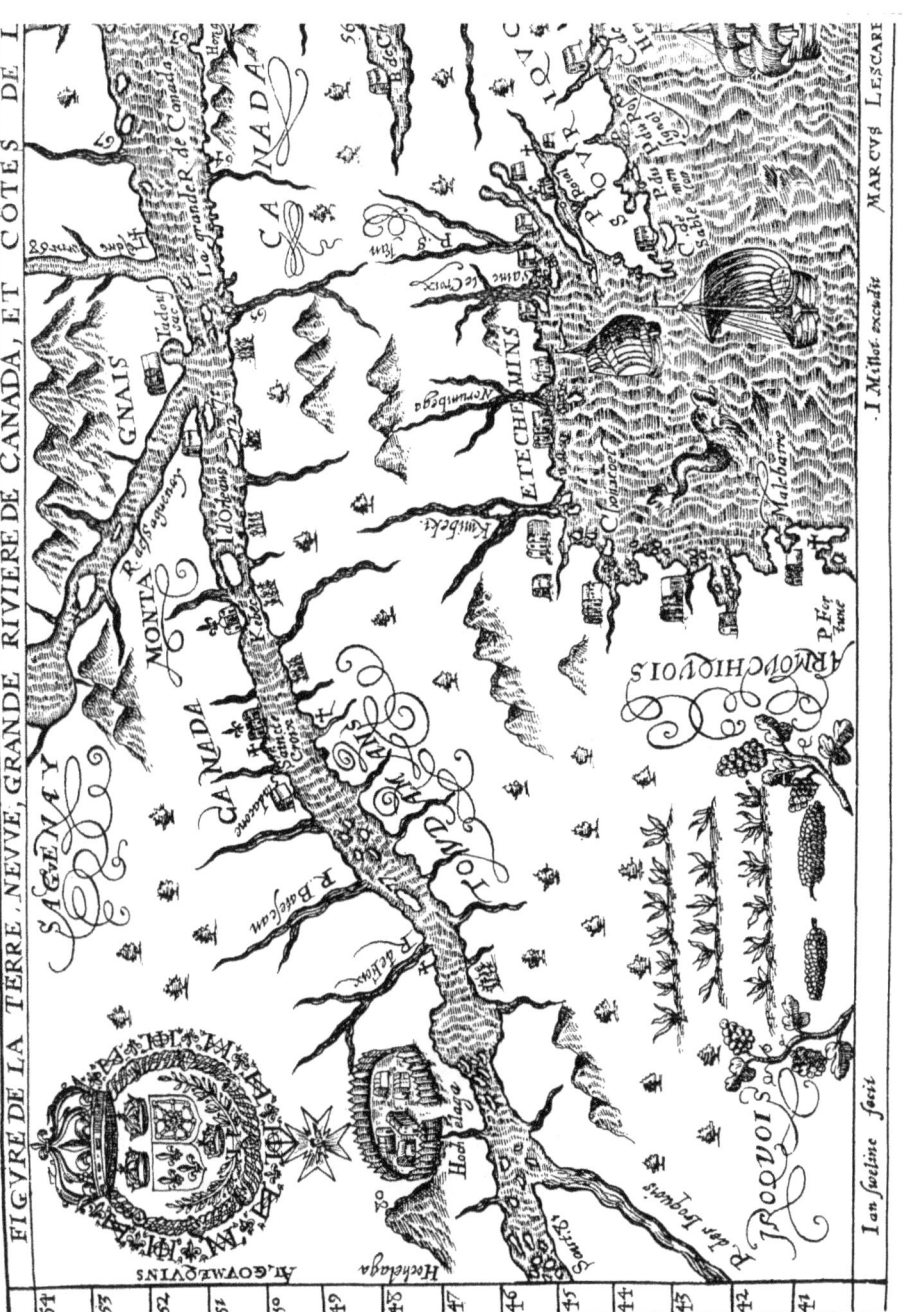

Map by Marc Lescarbot

Becancour, and the Chaudière, which head in the same highlands, are much shorter and tend to converge near Quebec. The Chaudière has carrying places to all the important rivers of Maine and New Hampshire and enters the St. Lawrence just upstream from Quebec City. The Reverend Paul Coffin in 1797 wrote: "I was told a man may walk in a half a day on the waters of the Chaudière, Connecticut, Androscoggin, and Kennebec rivers. Farmers sometimes fetch seed wheat from Canada through the Chaudière and Dead River."

During the colonial era, France controlled all the carrying places to the heads of the New England rivers. With her firm alliance with the Indians of Maine and Canada, she as much as owned the wilderness, without the cost of expensive labor or of permanent settlements, and reaped an annual harvest of priceless pelts. Instead of forts and soldiers, a single Jesuit among a tribe of Indians secured the land and the trade that went with it for France. The French census of 1688 shows that from the Penobscot to the St. Croix, both inclusive, there were scarcely forty-five French in all eastern Maine, including women, children, and servants; yet no English could enter and settle there until after Quebec fell to the British in 1759.

As long as France could maintain her outposts, euphemistically called "missions," far down the rivers of Maine at strategically located spots like Fryeburg, Norridgewock, Castine, and the Bay of Fundy, she held complete sway over the area of Maine.

Chapter Four

Canoeing, Camping, Carrying and Castor canadensis

The Indian canoe traveler had to spend at least half of his time in a canoe going upstream, and they used setting poles to stem the current. The length of a serviceable pole varies with the depth of the water which, in turn, is dictated by the time of year. A "spring pole" is longer than a "summer pole." In the spring the water in the rivers and streams is much deeper, and a pole of twelve to thirteen feet is necessary, but in the low water of midsummer, poles of eight to ten feet are very good. Using paddles in shallow, rocky waters can damage the thin hardwood blades and was taboo with canoemen, because a good paddle is very hard to make by hand.

"What in the hell do you think you are doing?" an old timer I know yelled at a novice canoeist who was using the guide's best paddle to push a canoe over a rocky ledge. "Would you take a Stradivarius violin and slam it into a brick wall? No, of course you wouldn't," he answered rhetorically. "Well, don't use my paddles to pole a canoe!" The analogy indicates what he thought of his paddles and hints at the time and effort he put into hand crafting a good paddle. Poles are meant for pushing, snubbing and prodding, but paddles only for paddling. The Indians, with stone and bone tools, took great care with their paddles and used poles whenever necessary.

One seldom sees a canoeist equipped with setting poles today. I have met people who have expressed feelings from disbelief to profound sympathy when they observed me poling up the West Branch or some other river. Once at Chesuncook Lake a woman who found out that our destination was twenty-two miles upriver at Northeast Carry and that we had naught but pole and paddle said,

"You poor man " and she meant it! I thought that I was having a good time, but she thought my pastime was a sort of torture.

On the rough East Branch Penobscot, a funny incident occurred when I poled my twenty-foot Smart canoe past a group of Rhode Island canoe buffs who had crunched to a stop on some sharp rocks.

"You can't stand up in a canoe," the head man helpfully offered as we said hello. "We learned at the YMCA," he continued, "that you should be on your knees at all times you're going to tip for sure." He said this out of a sense of duty rather than with the firm expectation that I would pay any attention.

Another asked our destination and was told that it was upstream at Matagamon Lake, where they had put in. "Well how are you going to get there?" she then asked, oblivious to the fact that we were poling past them as they pulled their dented aluminum canoes off the rocks. I said that I expected to pole the whole way and carry past the falls. They looked on in disbelief, and, as the twenty-footer slid around an upstream corner, the dented aluminum fleet from Chuck's Wilderness Outfitters, Cranston, Rhode Island, was getting back underway and arguing about the merits of standing in a canoe, and whether I knew what I was doing, or if I was as green as they were.

Poling a canoe upstream requires coordination and determination, especially when learning. Anyone who has learned to pole a canoe can recall embarrassing moments when the pole has wedged between rocks so securely that he had to let go of it, or break the pole, and maybe fall into the water in the process. This happens to everybody, and the prudent canoeist simply reaches down and picks up the spare pole that should be there.

Many funny stories, and some sad, begin when the spare pole isn't there.

Rocks and shallow water were very dangerous to fragile bark canoes, but they are easily spotted when standing up to pole or paddle and more easily avoided. Don't take me wrong, there are definitely times to be seated or kneeling in a canoe, but what my friend from Chuck's didn't realize was that an ascent of the East Branch is not one of those times.

When poling, the canoeist looks for the various natural river

4. Canoeing, Camping, Carrying, and Castor canadensis

features that will be helpful; rocks help the upstream canoeist, as they create eddies, or swirls of negative current, just below the rock. Eddies are used by the canoeist like stairs. That is, he poles the canoe from one eddy to another, keeping out of the strong current whenever possible. When I was learning to pole, Myron Smart told me, "The easier you are working, the better you are going." At first this baffled me, but, after I had begun to get the idea of poling, I understood that he meant that as my skill in poling and reading the water developed I would use less and less energy. These skills, making a canoe do what you want it to, allow one to keep the canoe in the easiest channel and, like the water, seek the path of least resistance, only in the opposite direction.

The rocks, then, create "stairs" in their eddies that break up the current and pull the canoeist up behind the rock or along the shore

Photo Margaret Cook

as he seeks out the next rock, ledge or bend in the channel and the helpful eddy swirling just below.

Canoe travel is only practicable during the ice-free months of the year. It is not uncommon today for the ice to remain in the lakes of northern Maine until early May, although the rivers and streams are usually open before the lakes and ponds. The annual freeze-up comes in late November or in December even in "warm" winters, and in winter the Indian traveler could make straight for any point he wanted over frozen rivers and lakes, hauling his toboggan or moose sled behind. Snowshoes were important to winter travel, and Indians took advantage of the deep snows.

During the time that the Indians traveled the rivers in canoes, they had many favored campgrounds. The archaeological remains of these places show that different prehistoric cultural groups often chose the same places, undoubtedly for the same reasons. The Indians had to live off the land and had to supply some of their daily needs from the various animal and plant foods which they found along the way. Most of the traveling in the prehistoric period was by family groups, whose small requirement for food would not strain the available resources.

Prehistoric canoeists chose campsites that often still appeal to us. Their preferred campgrounds had a spring close by and, except in the cases of mountain quarry sites, were always on a body of water. These places have a good exposure to the sun and usually receive whatever breeze is blowing. Visibility was important for security reasons, and most of the old campsites have good views of

4. Canoeing, Camping, Carrying, and Castor canadensis

their approaches. Many of the place names that have come down to us memorialize a distinctive feature of such old campgrounds: Cobbosseecontee, "where they spear sturgeon by torchlight"; Machias, "bad little rapids"; Mattawamkeag, "at the mouth a gravel bar."[1] Such names noted available food, a geographic peculiarity, or the "canoeability" of a place.

The inexperienced camper supposes that one can camp anywhere in the Maine woods, but the experienced know better. I have traveled for miles hoping to find a place to settle for the night—but, sometimes, found no suitable place to pitch a tent or build a fire. Good campsites may be already occupied or the shore may be too low and wet, sure to be inhabited by various types of pesky mosquitoes, midges and black flies. Some places may have too many dead trees to allow safe camping. These have been known to fall, even in windless weather, and kill or injure unsuspecting campers who imprudently bivouacked too close. It is a great advantage to know in advance just where one is going to spend the night.

When searching out a place to camp, I often choose a site that has been used for thousands of years. A cursory archaeological inspection often shows evidence of long use, and a recent canoe trip of mine on the Machias River is a good example.

In June of 1983 I camped at the foot of the carries past Little Falls and Great Falls of the Machias River on consecutive nights. Erosion has eaten into the sandy banks, and fire-cracked rock, chipped and flaked material, as well as pottery shards, littered the campsites, indicating that many people had camped at these places for hundreds, probably thousands, of years.

All rivers in Maine have places where the fishing is still excellent. On the major canoe routes such a spot is most assuredly an ancient campsite. These places are particularly evident when ascending a river in a canoe. The rapids that today require a portage are the same as they have been for the last few thousand years. Most towns have their old milldams, built over falls where Indians fished. The falls made the fish easy to catch for the Indian, and provided power for the mill wheels of pioneer industry, nuclei for many small towns.

Virtually all of the well-known Indian campsites had springs close by. There are many examples to select from: Abagadusset Point in Merrymeeting Bay was such a campsite and was known for its fine spring. Another large Indian campground was at the mouth of the Kenduskeag. The old, and now defunct, Exchange Hotel was built over it, and the water is now drained into the Kenduskeag. The campground is now paved over, part of an urban renewal "renovation."

Kenduskeag is a Maliseet word meaning "eel weir place" and hints at the value of the place.[2] The stream was also an important canoe route to the Kennebec watershed via the Sebasticook from the Penobscot. This site was visited in 1604 by Champlain, who described it.

An old campsite exists at the mouth of Schoodic Stream on the Piscataquis River in the county of the same name. The stream is from a large spring-fed lake, and the annual spring freshets have scooped a pool out of the mouth of the brook, which produces fine trout. The word "Schoodic," the name of that spot (and misapplied to the brook and lake), means "trout place," still a perfect description of the deep, cold pool. It also has a nice spring close by.[3] A preliminary archaeological survey done of the Piscataquis Ahwangan from 1981 to 1983 exposed a range of artifactual material from the recent historic back to the mid-Archaic, six thousand years ago. There was even a Plano-style, Paleo-era piece found on Pleasant River in Brownville.[4]

In the winter, travelers had to have spring water, which, coming from warmer subterranean depths, does not freeze. Many of these springs, as well as many of the small formerly beaver-plugged brooks, have been completely erased by the works of modern man. Many activities, such as clearing land by cutting the forests, draining swamps, laying sewer lines, and mining the glacial kames for gravel, have lowered the water table of many places.*

Most of the well-used campsites were equipped with a large and immobile log kettle. The Indians of early times had no portable

---

*The water table is the depth below the surface where water is first encountered when digging a hole.

4. Canoeing, Camping, Carrying, and Castor canadensis

kettles; their descendants traded fur for such valuable things. Says Nicholas Denys, who came to New France in 1632:

> All these kinds of roasts were only an entree to arouse the appetite; in another place was the kettle, which was boiling. This kettle was of wood, made like a huge feeding-trough or stone watering-trough. To make it they took the butt of a huge tree which had fallen; they did not cut it down, not having tools fitted for that, nor had they had means to transport it; they had them ready-made nearly all places to which they went.

Denys also described the method of construction. The Indians first burned one side of the log and then dug out the charred wood with stone tools until they had a depression suitable for cooking. Cold water and the meat were put into the hollowed log and red-hot rocks were dropped in until the meat was cooked to the broth they loved. "They always have a supply of soup which was their greatest drink . . . Above everything, the kettle has always seemed to them, and still seems, the most valuable article they can obtain from us."[5]

Though Denys is speaking of the Micmacs, the Indians of Maine must have done the same, because "stone boiling" was a widespread cooking technique in ancient times.

Many campsites along the short routes, like the Sebasticook, Piscataquis, or Aroostook, and especially along the coastal cutoffs on the numerous peninsulas of Maine's coast, must have been supplied with these kettles.

Carries

When the Indian canoeist came to any obstacle too difficult for pole or paddle, he took his canoe out of the water and carried it on his shoulders. He "carried by," as the old hunters would say. Paths around natural obstacles such as falls, or between watersheds, were established and were used by a nearly forgotten people.

The trails are rough and indistinct today, and lugging a canoe and wangan is very hard work. The ends of portage paths can be particularly bad, as they tend to change with different levels of water.

In 1853 Thoreau went across Moosehead in a birchbark canoe and portaged to the West Branch Penobscot over Northeast Carry. He watched while his Penobscot guide, Joe Polis, prepared for the carry:

> He prepared his canoe for carrying in this wise. He took a cedar shingle or splint eighteen inches long and four or five wide, rounded at one end, that the corners might not be in the way, and tied it with cedar-bark by two holes made mid way, near the edge on each side, to the middle cross bar of the canoe. When the canoe was lifted upon his head bottom up, this shingle, with its rounded end uppermost, distributed the weight over his shoulders and head, while a band of cedar-bark, tied to the cross-bar on each side of the shingle, passed round his breast, and another longer one, outside of the last, round his forehead; also a hand on each side rail served to steer the canoe and keep it from rocking. He thus carried it with his shoulders, head, breast, forehead, and both hands, as if the upper part of his body were all one hand to clasp and hold it. If you know of a better way, I should like to hear of it.[6]

Well, I know a couple of better ways to carry a canoe. One is on top of my pickup truck, and another is tied to the pontoon of a Cessna 180, but these are not always available, even today.

For those times when I have to carry, I follow Joe Polis's example, although I have substituted plastic lawn furniture webbing for cedar bark, and it works fine.

4. Canoeing, Camping, Carrying, and Castor canadensis

Photo Margaret Cook

The advantage of rigging up a tump and chest line is well worth the little time it takes. Using this method I save my arm strength and use my legs and spinal column to carry the perfectly balanced load. I can easily steer and balance the canoe with one hand, leaving the other free to carry something else, or more likely, swat the insects that always inhabit such places.

I know from my own experience that this is the most efficient way to carry a canoe through the woods; I am able to cover more distance between rest stops, and I feel much better when I get to the other side.

In Maine the carries are numberless because of the falls and rapids in the rivers, and also because the headwater brooks and ponds of all the systems lie so temptingly near to each other. This allowed the Indians to pass from one system to another with ease.

Carries, or as they say in Canada "portages" are of two types: past falls and rapids, and from one watershed to another.

Usually carry trails past falls parallel the river as closely as possible and are over hard and rocky ground. The falls are the result of water falling over rocky ledges, and the trails tend to be dry, rocky, and fairly easy to find. There are some exceptions to this, like the carry past Indian Pitch on Webster Stream, a headwater of the East Branch. This carry did not follow the stream down to Matagamon, but crossed over to the little East Branch Penobscot. The customary route around Grand Falls on the Penobscot, near modern Millinocket, provides another example. The route up the West Branch went up Millinocket Stream to avoid the long and rough carry by Grand Falls on the big river. The Fowler Carry went from Millinocket Stream over into Quakish Lake and back to the West Branch Penobscot, above the falls.

Carries between watersheds, on the other hand, were often very hard to find. When they were found, they were often long and wet, with difficult walking. One of the purposes for establishing a carry was to make the necessary lugging as short as possible over the easiest slopes. In Maine the rivers are not divided by ridges or high ground except on the northwestern border with Quebec. More commonly, the rivers head in level areas and run in different directions to the sea. Such is the character of the very difficult country in Hancock and Washington Counties, where the westerly-flowing tributaries of the Penobscot, easterly-flowing tributaries of the St. Croix, and the southerly-flowing Union, Narraguagus, and Machias rivers (along with their numerous branches) all rise in the same huge wilderness bog. The terrain is very wet, and the carries, or the ends of them, change with the amount of water available at a given time. Indians pushed their canoes up a shallow "logan" as far as possible before they heaved them onto their shoulders.

Unlike portage routes that parallel a river or stream and are easy to follow, these trails strike off cross-country, over very difficult terrain, to make canoe connections with other important routes or places. These routes cannot be reasoned out but would have to be learned like a lesson and would be impossible for a beginner to cope with.

It is strange to think that the headwaters of our rivers are in low land, but this does not necessarily mean near sea level. In Maine the rivers flow from an elevated plateau that is high above sea level.

Today most of the old carry paths between watersheds are overgrown and obscure from disuse. Even in the old days when

4. Canoeing, Camping, Carrying, and *Castor canadensis*

these routes and trails were used, they were rough and indistinct. Thoreau complained about the difficulty of following the main East Branch carries. He said he could only distinguish the trail from the encroaching vegetation by seeing the marks made by the river drivers' spiked boots on the rocks and dead wood. He was hoping to find a clear path through the woods.

Such clear and open paths were not the fashion of Indian times. The trails were narrow because the Indians always walked in single file. The Indians wanted to keep their carry trails obscure and difficult, because they were afraid they would be used by their enemies, the Mohawks. In 1760, while portaging past shallow water on La Rivière Linière, a Chaudière River tributary and important segment of the canoe route to the Penobscot, Colonel John Montresor, the British military engineer, wrote:

> The Abenaquis, jealous of the knowledge of their country took care to leave but few vestiges of their route. Even here we found but few knotches on the trees, commonly called blazes, the savages' constant guide in the woods ... our first day's journey from the forks [of the Chaudière], the country was as barbarous as can be imagined.

This expedition was five days going about fifteen miles. Montresor was traveling in mid-June, after the spring melt had flowed away and he wistfully noted:

> On the melting of the snow it is no uncommon thing to go from the forks or crotch of the Chaudière to the carrying place [of the Penobscot] in two days, though the stream must then be so rapid and the channel is so full of rocks that it cannot but be very difficult and dangerous.[7]

The old carries were neither smooth roads nor easy to follow. Not a rock was removed from them; fallen trees were rarely cut away; long wet swales often could not be avoided. Travelers got over or around or under the obstructions as best they could, and they were in danger of losing their way. Anyone carrying a canoe struggled on with his burden as best he could with the canoe catching in the branches along the path, while his feet stumbled over boulders or slippery tree roots.

In 1773 another explorer, Hugh Finlay, looking for an overland route from Quebec to New England, wrote of the carry from the Chaudière to Penobscot Brook (Range 4, Township 3 NBKP on Maine's northwestern shoulder): "Then we took up our canoes and packs and walk'd S. by E. about 5 miles over bare roots of trees so interlaced and twisted that they resemble the skin of a corded melon."

I can hardly do better than to quote Finlay's description of their crossing the height of land between Portage Lake in Canada and Penobscot Lake in Maine for a good picture of woods travel in colonial days.

> 19th September, 1773. Three Indians carried each man a canoe three were loaded with pork flower (sic). Kettles and hatchets; the rest of the party carried fusils, powder and shot, paddles, blankets and all our remaining baggage; thus we set forward in Indian file keeping a S. by E. direction, we immediately lose the brook, it is on our left. The way is much more obstructed by fallen trees, large stones, and there's some miry places in it; we continued on a gently ascent 5 miles and cross'd the brook, we descend gently half a mile to the lake from whence the brook issues; we took nine hours to walk 9 miles. The branches of the trees tore and bruised our canoes, the boughs caught our packs, and so entangled us that at times we could not disengage ourselves for minutes, we scrambled over, and sometimes crept under fallen trees; tangled shrubs catch'd our feet and threw us down under our burthens; we had a most fatiguing march. After refreshing ourselves and mending our canoes, we embarked on still transparent water covered with bullrushes . . . we landed at the left corner of the end of this straight, took up our burthens as before and march'd a mile and walk'd a 1/4 mile further on a descent to a lake, the course S.E.
>
> Half way over this carrying place is just the height of land between Canada and New England.

Hugh Finlay, appointed surveyor of post roads, in 1773-74 traveled all the way from Quebec, up the Chaudière to Rivière Linière, and continued upstream to the Linière headwaters which rises close to the Penobscot watershed, which also rises on the Maine-Quebec boundary. They carried over to Penobscot Lake and then began their descent of Penobscot Brook. After a hard go below the lake they reached the South Branch of the Penobscot to the West Branch Penobscot, from which they carried over to Moosehead Lake via Northwest Carry. They paddled south to the West Outlet and the Kennebec River. Finlay's objective was to determine the route for a post road between Quebec and New England.

His nine-mile carry was made during late summer when the brooks were low. In higher water the carry is but a half mile.

These are contemporary descriptions of one of the most important major routes in Maine. At that time Quebec could be reached from the south only by a circuitous sea voyage, or by one of the overland routes. Even though the Indians had used these routes for centuries they had evidently not removed a stick or stone from the portage paths and were jealous to keep them secret. Improvements were made along many carry trails when the lumber era opened up the Maine woods in the nineteenth century. Oxen and later horses required better paths than the Indians had ever wanted.

Often these unimproved portage routes were very hard to follow and once lost could be impossible to find. One good account of just such an experience is found in the record left by an early French missionary, Father Gabriel Druillettes.

In 1646, over one hundred years before Montresor or Finlay, Father Druillettes left Quebec with an Indian guide for the Kennebec where he would establish a Catholic mission. He traveled by canoe over the same route that Montresor and Finlay would use: up the Chaudière and then, by portage, over to the Penobscot before reaching the Kennebec at Moosehead Lake.

Gabriel Druillettes was a saintly man and a devoted missionary. At this time the Mohawks were coming from New York to attack the Indians of Maine at the behest of their Dutch allies. Father Gabriel labored to protect the Maine Indians, allies of France, from further Mohawk depredations and spent much of his first winter in New England at Massachusetts Bay, treating with the Puritans on this matter.

Before he arrived on the Kennebec, he had a hard experience. While carrying from the Chaudière watershed, the guide mistook the route, probably at Portage Lake in Quebec, and steered too far north. Instead of finding the carry to Penobscot Brook, he probably found the Southwest Branch of the St. John River. J. A. Maurault, in his *Histoire des Abénakis,* says it was fifteen days before they came out near Madawaska, almost starved to death. From there they had another canoe journey of twenty-three or twenty-four days before they finally got to Norridgewock on the Kennebec. In all they traveled at least thirty-eight days coming from Quebec to the Kennebec. With good luck and good water conditions, Indians often made this trip in about five days.

In March of 1652 Druillettes made a winter trip. He and his guide returned to Quebec on snowshoes this time using the Kennebec/Dead River approach to the Chaudière, later made famous by the Arnold expedition in the Revolution. They met with several delays along the way and as a result were ten days without food. Maurault says that they boiled their moccasins and caribou hide camisoles to make broth. They also boiled their snowshoe strings which "tasted good" according to Druillettes. The leggings were not tanned moosehide, but rawhide "mooseshanks" which hunters preferred for snowshoe travel, since snow does not adhere to rawhide as it does to tanned leather. This trip took a month, and when they reached Quebec in April, they were again famished and half-dead from exhaustion.[8]

In the winter of 1760 Colonel Montresor arrived at Topsham after a terrible winter trip from Quebec he too fought off starvation by eating his moosehide pouches and leather strings. As soon as he was in fit condition, he was ordered back to Quebec to lead another expedition in June from Quebec to New England. His mission was to locate a potential road route that the British government wanted to build to connect Quebec lately wrested from the French with New England. This hardy officer went back and forth between

4. Canoeing, Camping, Carrying, and Castor canadensis

Quebec and Massachusetts Bay three times in six months on official business. Montresor's accounts and those of others like Druillettes give us some notion of the travel difficulties common in the woods of colonial Maine and Canada.

Castor canadensis

North American beaver (*Castor canadensis*) were great allies of canoe people. Beavers dam small streams and raise the water where it is shallow, or running with considerable current. These are like canals for canoeists. The dams are low and small, only two to three feet high. Ordinarily this is all the head that is needed to flood the low ground back to where the beavers find a new supply of wood to float down to their houses.

In a stream with considerable pitch, a series of small dams creates pools covering sharp rocks. It is relatively easy to slide or lift canoes over beaver dams, and they are easier obstacles to overcome than low water.

Sometimes beavers built dams which were very long and very high, creating large ponds which grew larger over the years. A part of the Northwest Carry, at the head of Moosehead Lake, was greatly shortened by a beaver dam which created a small pond and meadows. In 1760, Montresor spoke of seeing the beaver dam which was twelve feet high. By the Indian name Quorbeduk, recorded in 1764, Joseph Chadwick shows that the same dam still existed. This is now entirely flowed out by the great artificial lake at Seboomook, and but for these records and old maps, we should not know a part of that carry's history.

The very long carry of seven miles from Caucomgomoc Lake, "Big Gull Lake," on the Penobscot, to Baker Lake on the upper St. John, started from a small beaver pond on tiny Avery Brook, which runs into the head of Caucomgomoc Lake.[9] In 1858 Manly Hardy spent nine weeks near there and knew the ground perfectly. He said that the dam was small and the pond so shallow that he had seen a bittern standing near the middle of it. Just thirty years later, in the late 1880s, the dam was higher and the pond much larger and deep enough to easily float a big canoe. By 1928, the pond was still larger and was dammed by lumbermen for river driving. In this way ponds were sometimes made in the course of ages.

By the late nineteenth century, beavers were nearly trapped to extinction. Today they are once again plentiful because of government protection and years of no beaver trapping. As the beaver population has rebounded they often revive old habitats. Just to give a concrete example, take the stream which enters the Penobscot from the east about opposite Eddington Bend, formerly called Mantawassuc Stream, and now Eaton Brook.*[10] Its western branch is called Fisher Mill Stream and its eastern branch, Phillips Mill Stream. The Fisher Mill Stream has a branch just before reaching the Holden Meeting House which is commonly called Pinchgut Brook and heads high up between Wiswell Hill and Blake Hill.

Fisher Stream itself heads a little before the Bagaduce Road (the old road to Castine) crosses the valley, while Phillips Mill Stream passes through the Hungry Meadow and rises further east. From the Penobscot River to their highest source, these streams were once full of beaver whose dams turned a continuous succession of small ponds and an insignificant watercourse into a fine little canoeing stream. With the exception of passing a canoe over a low dam every now and then, or a stretch of ripples like those where the Phillips Mill Stream crosses Eastern Avenue, it was good canoeing all the way. There were old beaver works on the very upper reach of Fisher Brook in the early twentieth century. On the Pinchgut Branch

---

*Mantawassuc "inlet." This name applies to a large pool near the mouth of the brook which was its distinguishing feature.

4. Canoeing, Camping, Carrying, and Castor canadensis

there were remains of old dams on the stream well up into the hill country. From these small brooks carries could be made to streams that would provide suitable routes to the Narramissic River and lower Penobscot, Holbrook Pond and the headwaters of Blackman Stream which joins the Penobscot at Bradley, Phillips Lake and the Union River. Thus, a small and today unnavigable brook provided alternative routes north and south to points on the Penobscot and east to within two miles of the important Union River.

The so-called Tannery Brook in Brewer, now almost totally effaced by the modern sewer system, was one long succession of beaver dams, and in the flat space between the road to Bar Harbor and the Green Point Road where there are now homes and dry fields there used to be an old beaver pond. The Indians camped at Pesutamesset, "seen only when near it," the campground at the mouth of the brook.[11]

Felt Brook, beyond Whiting's Hill on the old Bar Harbor Road was full of beaver. The whole country east of Bangor was a network of beaver puddles. Much of the alder ground in the state is due either to old mill ponds, deserted and grown up, or to beaver ponds, where one who knows the signs can still find traces of the old works.

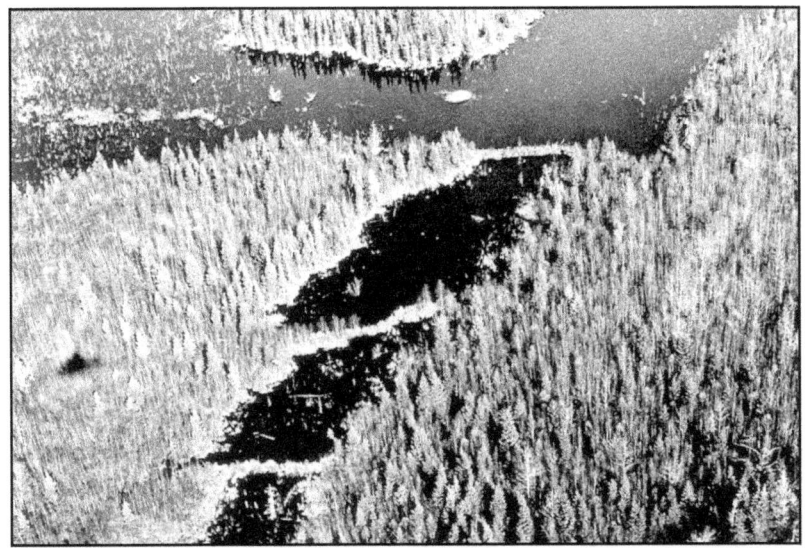

Beaverworks

It may seem needless to dwell so long upon conditions in one small locality, but there is no guesswork in speaking of this. Similar conditions were found all through the state in innumerable places. The topographical maps often show where in old times it is likely that the Indians were helped in their travels by the beaver. Chadwick called the beaver their only "domestic animals" except the dog, since they used them for furs and flesh just as we do herds of cattle, conserving the supply by judicious thinning every third year.

Old beaver ponds were free of obstructions for canoes because the dead wood and stumps had been rotted out by ages of flooding. In the old days canoe travelers often broke small dams open and allowed the water to run for an hour or so to fill up a small brook so that their canoes would float. The industrious beaver repairs the hole during the night to save the precious water for his own purposes.

Map by John Mitchell, 1755

Chapter Five

The Routes

The prehistoric canoe routes of Maine fall into four general categories: major routes, short routes, cutoffs, and neighborhood routes. While my concern is the river routes, ocean travel was also accomplished, as will be discussed below.

The major routes were along the great north-south rivers: the Saco, Androscoggin, Kennebec, Penobscot, St. John, and their major tributaries. These routes ended in some important place, such as a large town or tribal center, and they were used by tribal messengers and war parties. Later the Europeans used the major routes for quick communication with their frontier outposts and for exploration and survey work. The Jesuits have recorded that Indian couriers paddled the 430 downstream miles from Quebec to the mouth of the St. John in *five* days to deliver dispatches for the French. Such speed was only possible in times of high water and when traveling *with* the current.

The short routes went over the interconnecting tributaries and allowed direct travel between watersheds *when water levels permitted.* In the dry season many of the smaller streams become too shallow for canoes, and travelers are limited to the large rivers. Short routes were often segments in major routes, and they were used by the Indians for visiting neighboring regions and people.

The cutoffs were used for safety and convenience and are characterized by the numerous portage points that have been found on the coastal peninsulas. The ocean is very dangerous for canoes, and the carry paths across the long and narrow capes saved the paddlers dangerous passages through cold waters and high waves. All this is not to mean that prehistoric people did not travel on the ocean.

The final class of overland canoe routes is termed "neighborhood routes." They were byways through hunting and trapping regions, but had poor connections as canoe routes to any other place. There are many canoeable streams that lead nowhere but were important in the Indians' food-gathering cycle.

Many of these smaller streams have disappeared in the settled parts of Maine. Clearing the forests for farms and towns has lowered water tables and caused some of these smaller brooks to dry up. In the past these extinct water courses were dammed by beaver, whose dams and flowages helped the Indians penetrate into every nook and cranny of their territory.

Canoeing in the Gulf of Maine

In 1991 Professor Sanger visited archaeologists in Nova Scotia. He was interested in the artifacts which were found there, and he was seeking to find out more about the cultural connections, if any, between Maine and Nova Scotia.

Once there he met with colleagues who produced artifacts made of Kineo felsite and other types of rock which come from Maine. Sanger was also aware that in Maine relics were sometimes found that were made from a type of agate which only comes from Nova Scotia.

Upon seeing the first tray of artifacts Sanger thought his friends were trying to play a trick on him, since they were made from Maine material and of the distinctive "Moorehead Phase" which goes back in time over five thousand years.

He was assured that the artifacts had indeed been picked up in Nova Scotia, even though they were very similar to many Maine finds.

In thinking through this problem Sanger hypothesized that, since five thousand years ago, the people of both Maine and Nova Scotia were in contact with each other and that they most likely paddled their canoes across the Gulf of Maine. This statement caused some critical comments, since the Gulf of Maine and the Bay of Fundy have very dangerous conditions for small boats, because of the high tides and the exposure to open water. Some archaeologists argued that such trips were highly unlikely for those reasons and that the artifacts that Sanger had examined were probably transported by foot travelers. That would be a hike of seven hundred miles, and they still would need to have some means to cross the many rivers and streams which flow into the Gulf. Compared to a canoe voyage of less than one hundred miles, such a trip would be very daunting and time consuming. Imagine lugging a pack basket filled with Kineo felsite seven hundred miles to either trade or use as gifts once you arrived many weeks later.

It should be noted that some of the criticism came from folks with little actual experience in canoes and none of it on the ocean. The extensive archaeological sites out on Monhegan Island and the islands in Penobscot Bay are proof that people did navigate in salt water for thousands of years. On North Haven at the famous Turner Farm site, excavations revealed a sequence that goes back at least five thousand years.

The debate which Sanger precipitated gave rise to an ambitious venture which Mike Krepner initiated to prove such voyages were not only possible but highly probable. Mike contacted me and four other canoe enthusiasts with a proposal for a little "forensic archaeology" project; that is, he wanted us to paddle a canoe across the Bay of Fundy to demonstrate such trips were feasible.

Mike is a well-known canoeman and Master Maine Guide whose experiences have taken him all over the world. He has explored Maine's extensive waterways, as well as many others in both North and Central America. Mike is also a founder, along with Ron Canter and Randy Madres, of the 700-mile-long Northern Forest Canoe Trail, which extends from the far north of Maine across New England to the Adirondacks in New York State.

Mike also had spent much time in canoes in the Gulf of Maine, and he was quite sure that such a trip was possible, if prudence and safety were part of the plan. We all were excited about the opportunity Mike envisioned, and in August of 1998 we set out from Herring Cove, New Brunswick, with Nova Scotia fifty miles away on our minds.

Our first day was spent getting out to Grand Manan where we planned to camp one night before striking out for Nova Scotia. We had a 30-foot canoe and for safety were accompanied by a "chase boat." We all love canoeing, but all have a healthy respect for the ocean and the forty-five degree water of the bay.

Our stay on Grand Manan was extended one day by high winds, and we spent the day exploring the beautiful island which Mike has hiked all over in years past.

Our departure at 7 a.m. the next day was enshrouded by fog, but with calm conditions predicted, we struck off. We were in high spirits and eagerly dug our paddles into the cold waters. About one hour after we left, we encountered an interesting, and somewhat daunting, reality. As we paddled, we began to hear a noise that was similar to the sound water makes in a river as it runs over substantial rapids. The fog limited our visibility to a few yards, which probably amplified the noise.

As we continued, we realized that the rushing sounds were the result of the incoming tide. Our charts told us that the depth of the bay went from 50 feet deep to 500 feet, and the disturbance was responsible for not only the noise but also the four- to five-foot waves we suddenly found ourselves dealing with.

Mike's experience was valuable. He was in the stern of our canoe, steering so as to keep our canoe "quartering" into the chops. By taking the large waves on in a diagonal manner, we kept the length of our canoe in the water. To take such waves head on was to ship water over the gunwales which, if we took enough, would affect the way the canoe handled, as well as soaking us and our wangan.

After about an hour in such water, the sea calmed down and we were relieved. But high waves were not the only phenomenon we encountered.

The sea was no longer choppy but did rise and fall in large swells. Our canoe went up and down with the waves and, when we were at the bottom of one such swell we were rather alarmed to see a minke whale surface about 30 feet from our canoe and coming on fast, on a collision course.

The big animal was over thirty feet long and flat black in color;

it looked like a submarine. We were all transfixed by the creature, and there was no time to maneuver or even speak.

Just as the creature got within a few feet of us, with a great whooshing sound, the whale went under us, only missing our canoe by inches; I could have touched it with my paddle, although I did not even try.

That really got our attention, and we craned our necks nervously looking for more whales. Well, that was our only close encounter with such a critter, and we were glad. One of our crew, who spent much time on the Gulf of Maine's Hurricane Island, explained that whales are curious beasts, and he was just checking us out. "After all," he asked, "how many canoes has this, or any whale, ever seen out this far?"

Around two o'clock the clouds blew away and gave us our first view of Nova Scotia. Since we left on the incoming tide and were reaching Nova Scotia on the outgoing tide, our route across the bay was roughly S shaped.

At 5 p.m., after paddling through more rough water caused by exactly the same conditions we had already encountered, we pulled ashore in Whale Cove, Nova Scotia, ten hours after we left Grand Manan.

After we got ashore, I felt somewhat underwhelmed by it all. I do not mean that we were not impressed by the beauty and the power of the region, but I realized that if we could accomplish such a trip without real difficulty, so could people who were born and bred on the Gulf of Maine, who were very experienced and observed rules of their own, which made such a voyage safer. Remember, haste in such an environment might easily be deadly, and, just like today, some prehistoric people undoubtedly drowned when they encountered swiftly changing conditions. We had a big advantage: we listened to the weather reports issued several times a day by the National Ocean and Atmospheric Administration, which inform modern fishermen as well.

Our return trip was not in our canoe but aboard *The Cat,* the large and ultramodern ship which daily plies the Gulf of Maine between Maine and Nova Scotia at speeds of up to fifty miles per hour! We did prove such a trip was possible and, given the archaeological evidence, people had been doing the same for five thousand years just as Dave Sanger proposed.

Western Maine

In the western region of Maine, the Saco and Androscoggin rivers combine with the shorter coastal rivers, the Salmon Falls, Mousam, Presumpscot, and Royal, to link Maine's southwest coast with canoe routes to the interior in all directions.

The Saco watershed drains the eastern slope of the White Mountains and contains over 1,400 square miles, 800 in Maine.[1] From the main branch of the river, Indian travelers could reach the Merrimac/Lake Winnipesaukee district and the Connecticut River to the west, or the narrow Presumpscot system just to the east.

Sebago Lake, "the big lake," like other large interior lakes, was very important to the Natives and could be approached by canoeists from all directions.

The main Saco River, and its major branch the Ossipee, maintain good levels of water for canoe travel throughout the year. Tributaries such as the Little Ossipee, Kezar, and Cold rivers would have been used as short routes or perhaps neighborhood routes when the water was up.

The Androscoggin watershed contains 3,600 square miles, and twists 160 miles from the Rangeley Lakes through New Hampshire and back into Maine to join the Kennebec at Merrymeeting Bay.[2]

There were several important carries to salt water from the lower reaches of the Androscoggin, where the river runs west to east parallel with the coast. This section, near modern Brunswick, was called Pejepscot, "long rocky rapids part."[3] The Upper Carrying Place went from the main river, above Brunswick, south overland into Maquoit Bay. Further downstream below Pejepscot Falls, another carry left the river and went over into the tidal New Meadows River

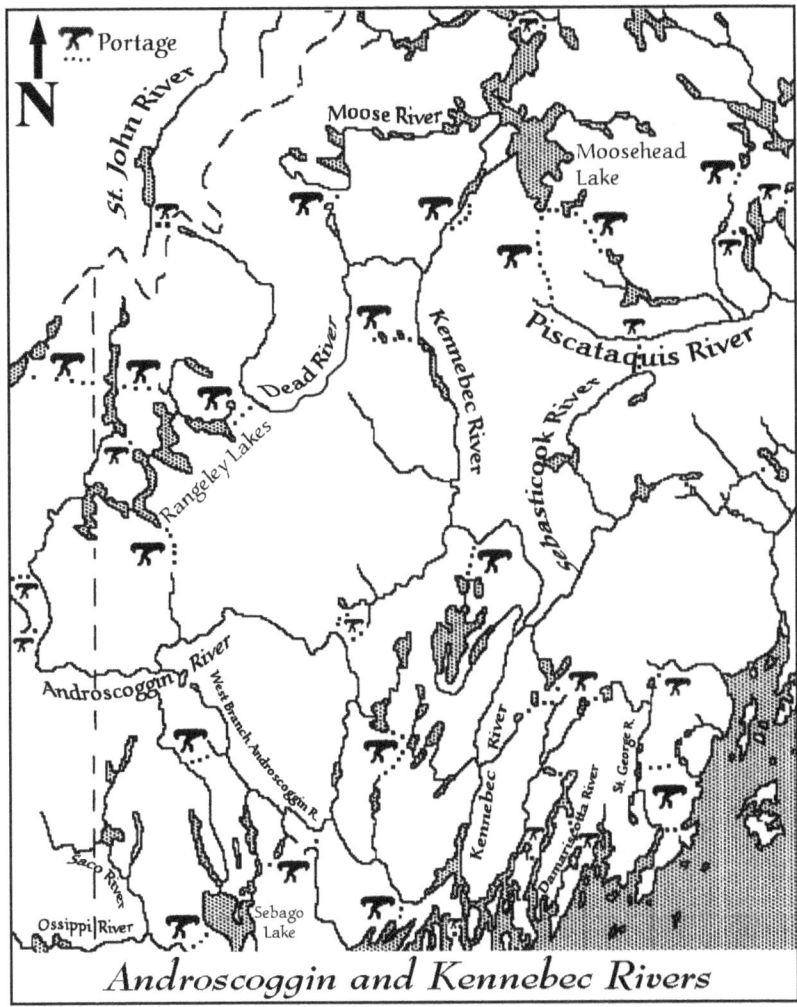

Androscoggin and Kennebec Rivers

and is still known as the Stevens Carry, after Thomas Stevens, an early pioneer, who owned the land in 1673.

The map shows many of the other natural portage points in the Brunswick region. In Topsham the principal portage was from the Androscoggin to Cathance Pond. It is highly probable that there was another portage at the head of Muddy River with connections to the Androscoggin and Cathance rivers.

From the lower Androscoggin travel to Sebago Lake and Casco Bay would have been easy and direct via the Little Androscoggin

River. When the canoeists desired to go to the Kennebec from the Androscoggin, they could ascend Sabattus Stream and make short carries into Cochnewagon Lake, "the closed-up route," and into the lakes of the Cobbosseecontee system on the Kennebec. The name "Cochnewagon" is a linguistic relic of the times when the Indians used it in their comings and goings. [4]

Another route from the Androscoggin to the Cobbosseecontee system was via Dead Stream into Androscoggin Lake. From this large lake, which has produced hundreds of stone artifacts from the last five thousand years, a short carry into Wilson Pond put the travelers onto Kennebec water, a short distance from Annabessacook Lake. Modern camp owners on Androscoggin Lake have found Indian artifacts where the old carry left the lake for Wilson Pond.

From the middle part of the Androscoggin River the Indian travelers could go directly north from the main river to the Rangeley Lakes by ascending Ellis River. This route saved a long westward swing through modern New Hampshire, but required a long carry from the head of Ellis River to reach the lakes. Other brooks, the Swift and Bear rivers, could have also been used but are more rapid and steep than Ellis River, and probably were used primarily as routes from the lakes to the main river when the water permitted and speed was required.

A route from the Rangeley Lakes to the Kennebec watershed went east from Rangeley Lake over short carries to the South Branch of the Dead River, a major Kennebec tributary and canoe route. Once in the South Branch, the travelers could descend to the Kennebec or push up Little Spencer Stream to eventually reach the Moose River drainage many miles above Moosehead Lake.

Routes from Aziscohos Lake via Dead Diamond River or Cupsuptic River went to the Connecticut River and the Lake Megantic region in the Chaudière watershed. The numerous connections, like those that the Androscoggin shares with the contiguous river systems, are common in canoe country.

Just east of the Androscoggin lies the Kennebec, the second largest river in Maine. The watershed encompasses 5,800 square miles and the main river is 145 miles long.[5] With 311 ponds and lakes, including Moosehead, Maine's largest lake, and its many subsidiary streams, the Kennebec had many excellent canoe travel opportunities for those who knew the lay of the land, or more appropriately, the flow of the waters.

The Kennebec runs into the ocean at Sagadahoc, "where the river runs in" (to the ocean), and wends its way through the many islands of the tidal sections.[6]

The canoe possibilities here defy description, but local maps do much to explain them. In this region numerous cutoffs were used over the narrow peninsulas and many of the coves are still called "Carrying Place Cove," and the reason is obvious.

Another example is the name Winnegance, which is applied to a bay in New Meadows River and a creek opposite on the lower Kennebec. The name means "the carry" and does not refer to either body of water, but to the intervening land that separates them.[7]

Merrymeeting Bay receives the water of three other rivers besides the Androscoggin and Kennebec. Although these rivers Cathance, Eastern, and the Abagadassett are not big, they were important routes for travelers and hunters alike.

The word "Kennebec," or "long water place," was meant to describe the quiet stretch of river from between the Chops (Kebec to the Indians "where the river narrows") to Taconic Falls.

Canoe travelers ascending the Kennebec had many interesting options to select from. Once above Merrymeeting Bay the canoeist could bypass the middle section of the Kennebec, from Cobbossee to Taconic, "where they cross," by going up Cobbossee Stream through its lakes and by carry, to the Belgrade Lake chain and then back into the main river.[8] It was also possible to ascend Worromontogus Stream and, by carry, reach China Lake and then by following the outlet, get back to the main Kennebec.

Travelers who used these alternative routes could parallel the main branch or go west to the Androscoggin, or east to the coastal Sheepscot River with connections to Sheepscot, Muscongus and Penobscot bays. Travel to the upper river would be faster and more direct on the main branch, but with the versatility of the interior routes the Indians could travel easily to maximize food and fur resources, as well as reach neighboring watersheds to the east and west.

Above Cushnoc, "the head of tide," at the old village of Taconic, the river branches in several directions.[9] The routes west via Messalonskee Stream to the Belgrade Lake chains and to the east, via Outlet Stream to China Lake, have already been mentioned. In the same vicinity the Sebasticook River, a major route, runs into the Kennebec from the east and had many links to various regions in the vast Penobscot drainage. Sebasticook, another Indian word relating to canoe routes, means "the short route" and is appropriate in describing the role of the river for the Native Americans.[10]

In traveling over the Sebasticook, Indians reached the following important Penobscot objectives:

- Unity Pond, Belfast, Passagassawakeag region, via Twenty-Mile Stream
- The lower Penobscot, below the head of tide, via carry to Souadabscook Stream
- The Bangor region via carry to Kenduskeag Stream
- The region around Old Town, above the falls, by carry into Pushaw Stream
- The upper Piscataquis River, the Piscataquis Ahwangan, into hunting and trapping territory as well as Moosehead Lake.[11]

Moosehead Lake could be reached by ascending the Kennebec, but this was a very hard route. Above The Forks the junction of the Kennebec with the Dead River the river is swift and falls through very rough terrain, making necessary long and arduous carries. Montresor came *down* this route in 1761 and nearly met with disaster. He described the East Outlet of the Kennebec on Moosehead and the danger for the canoeist.

> This river is considerable from its first source. Its breadth is about one hundred and fifty yards; its depth more than required for canoes. Being used to suffer from the shallowness of the

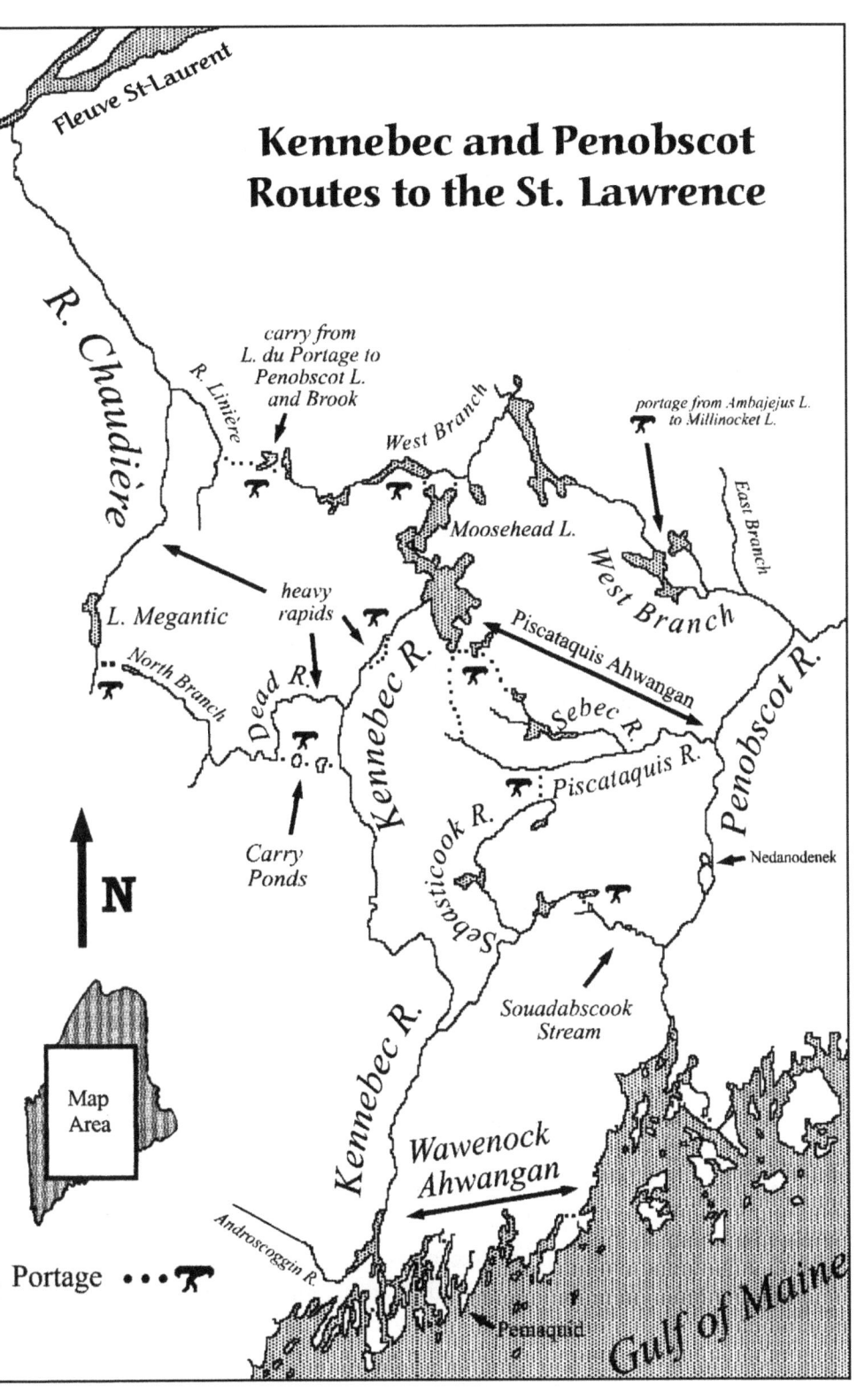

difficulties we were to meet with. Having gone a little way with great velocity, all at once we found ourselves engaged in rapids. The river was narrow, deep and full of rocks. To go back or gain the shore was equally impossible. One of the canoes overset; all the rest filled with water, but with much difficulty we gained the shore. Our provisions being all wet and in danger of being lost, we were obliged to encamp. We had not the consolation of better prospect before us, for along the bank, as well as in the river, there was nothing to be seen but rocks; the woods filled with spruce, cedars, and certain marks of a country good for nothing. The descent every where so great, that the river runs with vast rapidity.[12]

After they repaired their canoes, they set out again and by what Montresor referred to as the "great dexterity" of the Indians, avoided a repetition of the accident just recounted. When they reached the foot of Indian Pond, today greatly enlarged by a dam, Montresor's party took a carry path that left the eastern side of the pond and went a short distance east to a small stream still called Carry Brook:

Upon this creek we advanced four miles, and opened a vast number of beaver dams, which were of some use to us. It seems the Governor of Canada had been formerly acquainted with this, and all hunters were by his edict forbid to molest the beavers in this part of the country.[13]

The detour away from the dangers of the Kennebec to Carry Brook is a good example of a canoe route following the easiest course. This brook parallels the river and, when plugged by water-saving beaver, could be used as a canoe canal. Montresor's guides avoided a very hard portage over the extremely rough course of the main Kennebec by opening beaver dams and wading their loaded canoes down this small brook.

Moosehead Lake was also reached from the Dead River system during high water. Montresor's guides told him that the descent of

5. The Routes: Western Maine

Snubbing down through a sharp set of rapids

the Kennebec from Moosehead was safer in high water because they "could keep close to shore without being in the rapidity of the current." This means the Indians used setting poles and gently "snubbed" their canoes downriver. In the low water of July, Montresor and his Indian guides were forced to stay in the deepest and swiftest channels where danger of swamping is the greatest.

For the upstream canoeist the upper Kennebec, in high water or low, is difficult and this makes alternative routes like the Dead River/Spencer Stream connection to the Moose River very attractive. You can commonly run a canoe down through rapids too rough to pole up through, and to reach Moosehead Lake from The Forks required difficult carries along the shore and an ascent of Carry Brook. Once at Indian Pond the easiest route to Moosehead is up West Outlet Stream. It is smaller and easier to ascend than the large and swift East Outlet.

For those coming downriver, the main Kennebec is (except for the flowages behind the big dams at Caratunk and Skowhegan) as Montresor described it, rough but practicable.

Wesserunsett Stream, entering the Kennebec from the east, is also part of the old network of Kennebec canoe routes. This fine fishing stream was used as a way to and from the Piscataquis region which drains the large bog region at the foot of Moosehead Lake.

Another tributary route was the Carrabassett, today famous as a whitewater canoe run. This rapid stream can be canoed in the right stage of water, but is very difficult when compared to neighboring Sandy River.

The Sandy is much more commodious for canoeing. It has a gentle pitch over its distance, and provides a direct Kennebec/Rangeley Lakes/Androscoggin canoe connection. At Farmington Falls, the Indian village of Amascontee, "plenty of alewives," was an easy canoe trip from Norridgewock on the main Kennebec.[14] The Carrabassett has long and thundering rapids, while the Sandy meanders through a broad and fertile valley with canoe connections to the Belgrade/Kennebec lake system.

The Dead River is the last major route leading from the main Kennebec. This was the route of Arnold's march on Quebec during the Revolutionary War and was an ancient route at that time. Arnold's information about the route came from Montresor's interesting report written in the 1760s. I have already explained how this route left the Kennebec below The Forks and went northwest through the Carry Ponds to the Dead River. From the Dead, canoeists connected with the Androscoggin, or Chaudière headwaters, by carry over into Moose River from Spencer Stream. Indians who knew the route could completely avoid the rough section of the Kennebec below the lake by ascending into the Dead River country and then, by Spencer Stream, reach the Moose near Attean Pond, detouring by the lakes. If the goal was the region above Moosehead, then this short route was a good choice. It would be hard traveling in places, but they are mild when compared to the dangers and difficulties of the Kennebec, especially if the water was high.

Moosehead Lake was important to the Native Americans of the northeast coast and woods for several reasons. First, Moosehead, like Sebago and other large lakes, was a travel hub for major canoe routes to and from the neighboring river systems. Second, Mount

Kineo, rising from the east shore of the lake, is the source of felsite, a volcanic rock like chert, which oozed up through the earth's crust some 425 million years ago. Felsite, mistakenly called flint there is no flint native to Maine was used by the Indians for tools and weapons for many thousands of years.

Montresor noted another Moosehead Lake important resource: "For the birch, of the sort most valued, the banks of this lake are particularly famous."[15] The Indians used birch bark for houses, buckets, and baskets, as well as canoes.

The final reason for Moosehead's great significance was the hunting, trapping, and fishing opportunities of the region.

Unfortunately, many of the artifacts left by the Indians have been lost to history for several reasons. Moosehead has been a resort for tourists for over one hundred years, and as a result much of the archaeological material has been found and portaged out of state long before there ever was any sensitivity to the importance of such matters. I was told by Elizabeth Hartshorne, who was raised on Northwest Carry during the 1920s and '30s, that in her father's hotel, The Northwest Carry House, there was a collection of "five thousand perfect pieces mounted in picture frames and hung on the walls." This hotel was used during World War II to billet German prisoners of war, mostly members of Rommel's famous Afrika Korps, who had been put to work cutting pulp in the north woods. According to Mrs. Hartshorne, "those devils burned it down," which destroyed the artifacts.

There are many other such tales of Moosehead artifacts found, only to be lost again. For many years a man from New Jersey summered at "the Lake" and dug up and took home thousands of artifacts from the vicinity of Sand Bar Point. How many others, fascinated by the abundance of Indian weapons and tools, did the same? What would they add to our knowledge of prehistory if they had been properly curated?

Another problem is that the modern dam at the outlet of the lake has raised Moosehead's water levels and inundated archaeological sites closest to the shore. The industrial activity over the last hundred years, and the relic hunters, have had a severe impact

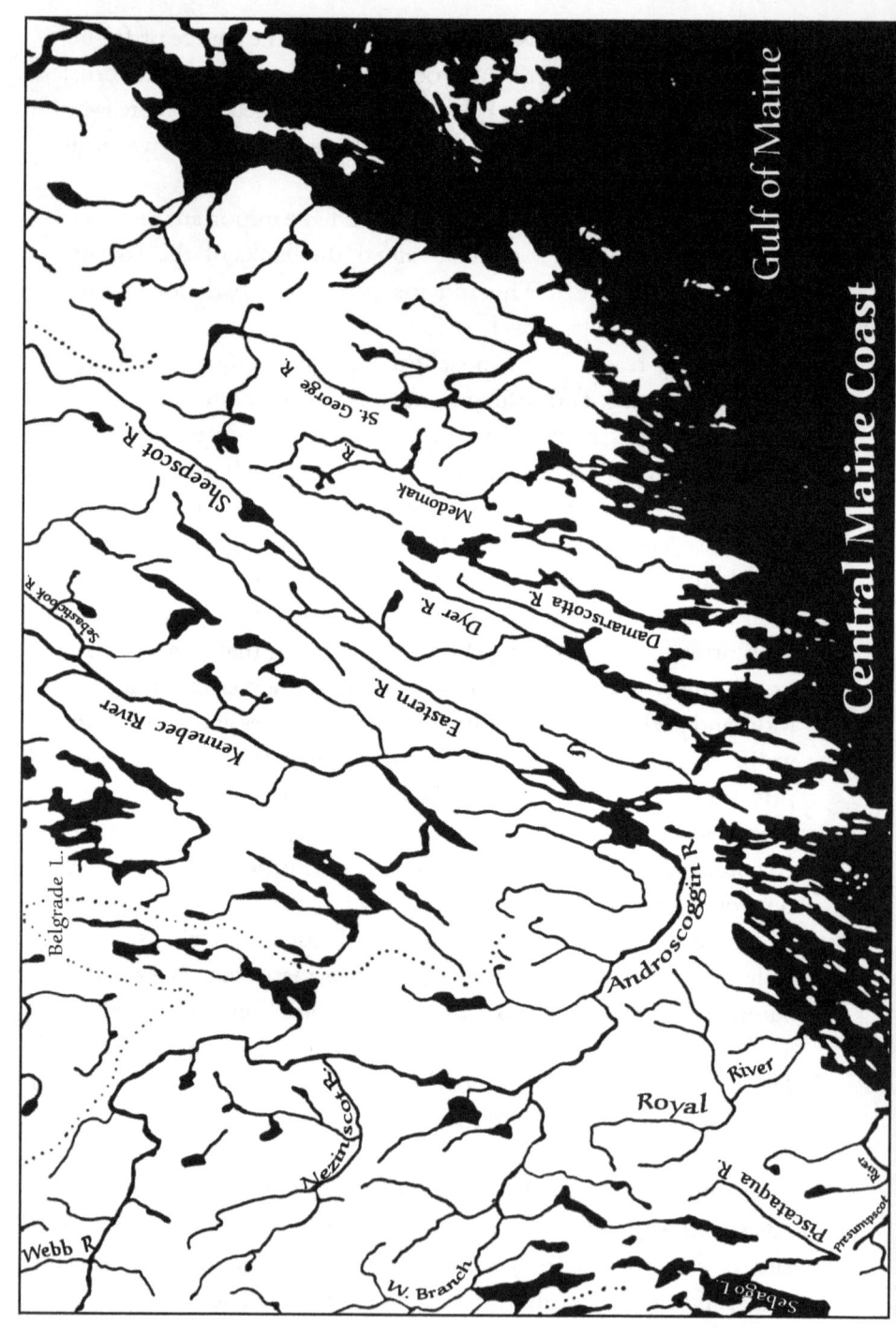

on the archeological record of this major interior canoe crossroad. If many of the collections from Moosehead could be located and systematically studied they would undoubtedly reveal a long and multicultural history. The incidence of Kineo felsite in archaeological materials throughout the Northeast indicates that it was important. Perhaps, as Prof. Bonnichsen hypothesized, the Indians had developed a sophisticated trade in these lithic resources, as they most surely did with Munsungan cherts.*[16]

Mid-Coastal Canoe Routes

The mid-coastal region from the Kennebec to the Penobscot, like the rest of the Maine coast, has many excellent canoe routes. The Eastern, Sheepscot, Damariscotta, Medomac, and St. George rivers all rise in the area south of Souadabscook Stream, a Sebasticook/Penobscot canoe route. These rivers roughly parallel each other and outlet in the ragged coastal region so popular with tourists today. Many tourists would be surprised to know just how long people have been going there for clams, lobsters, and cool sea breezes.

These rivers are all connected by portages and are easy canoeing. They do have occasional falls and rapids where the Indians carried their canoes, or camped to fish for some of the various types of anadromous fish sturgeon, salmon, alewives, and shad that used to fill these streams in their season. Here, white man built his dams, mills, and eventually, towns. Where the Indians used to catch fish, the Europeans used the falling waters to turn the wheels of industry to grind, saw, and hammer out the many products that became necessary on the Maine frontier.

While the towns, Whitefield, Coopers Mills, Jefferson, Appleton, and Union, remain, the water-powered mills have almost vanished,

---

*Outcroppings of rock used by the Native Americans as raw material in weapon and tool manufacture.

leaving their traces in greater abundance than the relics of the prehistoric people who lived there for thousands of years.

Characteristically, the easternmost of these rivers, the St. George, had several connections with Penobscot Bay along its length.

Indian canoeists used these coastal rivers west of Penobscot Bay to get to the ocean, or as an interior passage between the Kennebec and Penobscot Bay, and so avoid the dangers of coastal canoe travel.

Coastal Cutoffs

In the mid-coast region there are all types of canoe routes. Coastal cutoffs abound, and they were characterized by carries across peninsulas west and east of Penobscot Bay for good reason. Coastal canoeing is very dangerous. The rocky shores, strong tides, and sudden storms make travel difficult at best. The Indian canoe travelers sought the safest way and took advantage of the numerous options offered by the various rivers and lakes. These are situated in such a way as to afford interior canoe routes which parallel the ocean through good hunting terrain with no exposure to the ocean.

The many islands provide inside passages for canoes with protection from the wind along the coast.

At places like Pemaquid Point, open for miles to the sea, the coast was impossible for canoes. To avoid this dangerous stretch the Indians had a cutoff from the Damariscotta River to New Harbor, and another to Round Pond, and no doubt another higher up to Broad Sound.

The Indians had an inside route from Camden to Belfast. On the east side of Penobscot Bay, the coastal rivers provided interior canoe routes all the way to Lubec in extreme eastern Maine.

Suppose Indians wished to get from Bucksport on the west side of Penobscot Bay east to the Blue Hill region, and bad weather was expected. The route they would choose would be down the East River, as there is no great tide there. They would be exposed for a time along Penobscot Bay's Doshen shore to Castine Neck. The

5. The Routes: Coastal Cutoffs

carry across Castine Neck was most easily done at high tide, which accounts for the name, Edali-si-back emuck, "where they waited for the tide."*[17]

After waiting, the Indians carried into Hatch Cove on the Bagaduce River. If they did not want to go by Castine's fort and wanted to avoid treacherous Cape Rosier, they went between Holbrooks Island and Nautilus Island to Goose Falls and then crossed to Weir Cove. This was Edali-chichiquasik, "where it is very narrow."[18] This route saved them from exposure to the dangerous winds and strong tides of Cape Rosier, dreaded by canoeists. If going farther, they went up Lawrence Bay and across into Horseshoe Cove or Orcutt Harbor.

If they wanted to go farther down the coast to Eggemoggin Reach,[19] "the fish weir place," they went from Castine Neck by the Minnewokon, "the many directions route."[20] This route went by Bagaduce River to Walkers Pond and by a very short carry into the Punchbowl above Sedgwick.

Continuing down a very short stretch brought them to Benjamin River between Sedgwick and Brooklin. This route took them to Blue Hill Falls which, at times, is rapid in both directions, depending on the tides. Thus, they could reach their destination entirely protected from the sea and wind all the way from Bucksport, except for the Doshen Shore of Castine.

On the west side of the river they had several safe passages. A difficult paddle around Fort Point was avoided by the Ooniganissek, "the short carry," into Stockton Springs.[21] If they were continuing, they then went behind Sears Island (aka Brigadier's Island) into Belfast Bay. The Passagassawaukeag River, "the sturgeon place,"[22] leads up to Megunticook Lake, which gave protected access to Camden Harbor. This was also a route to St. Georges River and the section of the coast east of Penobscot Bay.

---

*This can easily be seen today. In fact the British attempted to canalize it and the remains may still be seen.

The Penobscot System

In the middle of the state of Maine the tributaries of the Penobscot River system fan out from the main branch so that the watershed spans the width of the state. It has headwaters on the Quebec border in the west, and on the border with New Brunswick in the east. The drainage contains 8,200 square miles, about one fourth of the entire state, and 1,604 lakes and ponds connected by streams many of them substantial rivers.[23] The Penobscot had more canoe routes than other Maine rivers, because it is the largest river basin, and it is in the center of the northeastern canoe route network.

We know more about these Penobscot routes because the Penobscot Nation is still extant, and many of Maine's early soldiers, explorers, and tourists, who left records traveled over at least a portion of the Penobscot drainage, if they went any distance in the Maine woods.

The major reason is that the people native to the region still reside on the banks of the Penobscot, and the names they applied to the region are far better preserved. On the Penobscot and to the east, the Indians remained on their lands. Even though they were engulfed by the dominant white culture and saw most of their tribal lands taken, they maintained themselves as a people, and as a result we know more of the Penobscot, Passamaquoddy, Maliseet, and Micmac.

Some of the routes to and from Penobscot Bay have already been mentioned in the previous discussion about the mid-coastal region and coastal cutoffs. There were, of course, others about which we know little today.

As one ascends the Penobscot by canoe many routes lie open in all directions. On the lower section, below the head of the tide, the river was called Pemtegwa'took which means "main river."[24] As mentioned, the Indians named only parts of rivers after a distinguishing characteristic. Many of the names for the lower part, as well as the upper sections of the Penobscot, have long since disappeared. Penobscot means "the rocky place" or "the descending

5. The Routes: The Penobscot System

ledge place" and was applied to the section above the modern dam in Bangor, at the head of the famous Salmon Pool, to Great Falls in Old Town.[25] It still describes this section very well, as it remains swift and rocky. Above Old Town the river was called Pannawambskek, "where the ledges spread out."[26] The valley and river both expand, the river being one thousand feet wide in places, flowing past lushly covered hardwood islands, maple being the predominant species.

The lower Penobscot, like the Kennebec, had parallel routes over which the hunter/trapper could travel if speed was not needed.

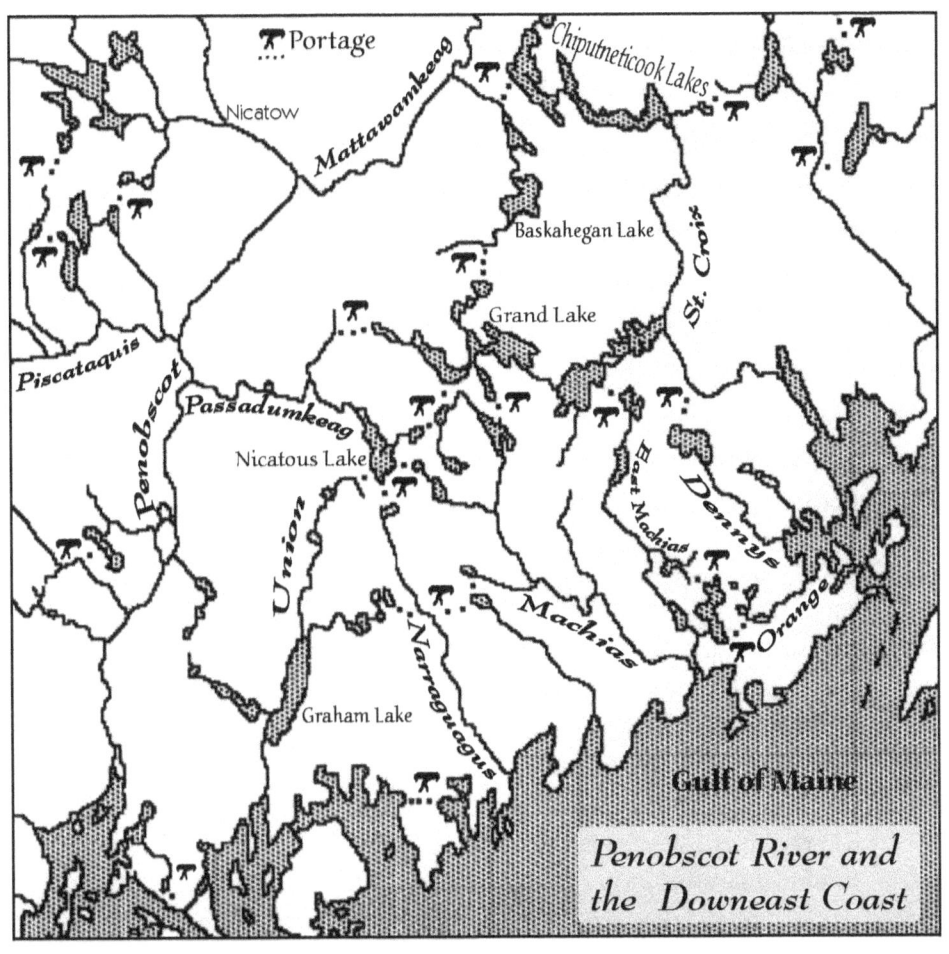

Penobscot River and the Downeast Coast

On the west side, for example, the canoeists went up Muskrat Brook, above Sandy Point and below Verona Island, and made a rugged carry over into the South Branch of Marsh River, which enters the Penobscot four miles above Verona Island, below Winterport, where the river expands to over one mile in width.

On the east side, the Orland River had canoe connections with Alamoosook Lake and Toddy Pond and from these to the lakes and ponds near modern Ellsworth and the Union River watershed, with its outlet on Penobscot Bay, near Mount Desert Island. Canoeists had a direct, interior route to the coast, well protected from foul weather.

One could also, by going up the Dead River/Moosehorn Stream waterway, connect with the lakes to the east, Phillips, Green, and Branch lakes, or carry north into what is now called Thurston Pond (Bucksport). From there they went downstream into Brewer Lake. From this lake, Sedgeunkedunk Stream, "rapids at the mouth,"[27] runs north to the Penobscot in Brewer near the ancient campsites of Pesutamesset, "seen only when near it,"[28] Kaghskibinday, "cedars,"[29] and downstream a short way from Kenduskeag, "the eel weir place,"[30] on the west side of the river.

Souadabscook Stream, "at the sloping ledge,"[31] coming in from the west, was a Sebasticook connection, and it enters the Penobscot five miles below Kenduskeag. Both were canoe routes, but the Kenduskeag is much the larger, draining ninety square miles.

The falls in Bangor, now the head of tide, used to be flowed out at high tide and the actual head of tide was Wabenobahntuk, "white water falls," upstream at modern Eddington Bend.[32] Both these places were favorite camping and village sites with the Indians. The point on the Veazie side was a Native American village called Negas,[33] which commemorated the portage across the point, and the place had been cleared by the Indians for agriculture. Later called Crowne's Point, after the first fur trader, this was the most important spot on the lower river. The Indians occupied the valley for ten miles on both sides in villages and smaller campgrounds, where they took advantage of the excellent hunting and trapping found all around.

Just above this spot Felt and Eaton brooks were excellent

5. The Routes: The Penobscot System

examples of neighborhood routes. These small and practically extinct brooks were once plugged full of dams by the beavers and were virtual canoe canals for the hunters and trappers who pushed canoes over them in search of game.

If a traveler at Negas wanted to go to the Union River country to the east, he would pole up the Penobscot five miles to Blackman Stream, which runs into the Penobscot from Chemo Lake, to a small chain of ponds with carries into the region near Graham Lake on the Union watershed. Above Orono other Penobscot/Union River routes help explain why the Union River was part of the Penobscot tribal domain when the Europeans arrived; they had direct access to Union River waters over the small but important Great Works Stream, Sunkhaze, and Olamon Stream, "red paint."[34] There was also a connection with the West Branch of the Union River on the Passadumkeag. These streams are better traveling in high water, but they were full of beaver.

In the Old Town-Orono area, the Penobscot River has created three large islands: Marsh Island (site of the towns of Orono, Old Town, and the University of Maine), Orson Island,* and a large island in the Penobscot above Old Town.[35]

In 1764, Joseph Chadwick was commissioned by the British government to "survey through the intereparts of the Countery from Penobscot to Quebec . . ." Like Montresor in 1761, Chadwick "was first to explore the Countery seccotly, to View if it were practicable to make a Road from Fort Pownall to Penobscot River to Quebec."[36] With John Preble as head guide, Chadwick went to, as he called it, "Ille of Penobskeag," the tribal headquarters of the Penobscot tribe, to hire the help of the Indians.

In a "Memorandem" Chadwick notes that the tribe was not enthusiastic about his work. As Montresor noted, the Indians were always secretive about their canoe routes and the Penobscots were also feeling the strain of changing times.

---

*Orson is an Indian family name found elsewhere in the Penobscot watershed. It is the Penobscot pronunciation of the French baptismal name of *Jean* or John. Pronounced "Aw-sawn," the name is also found in Orson Bog just west of Schoodic Lake, Piscataquis County.

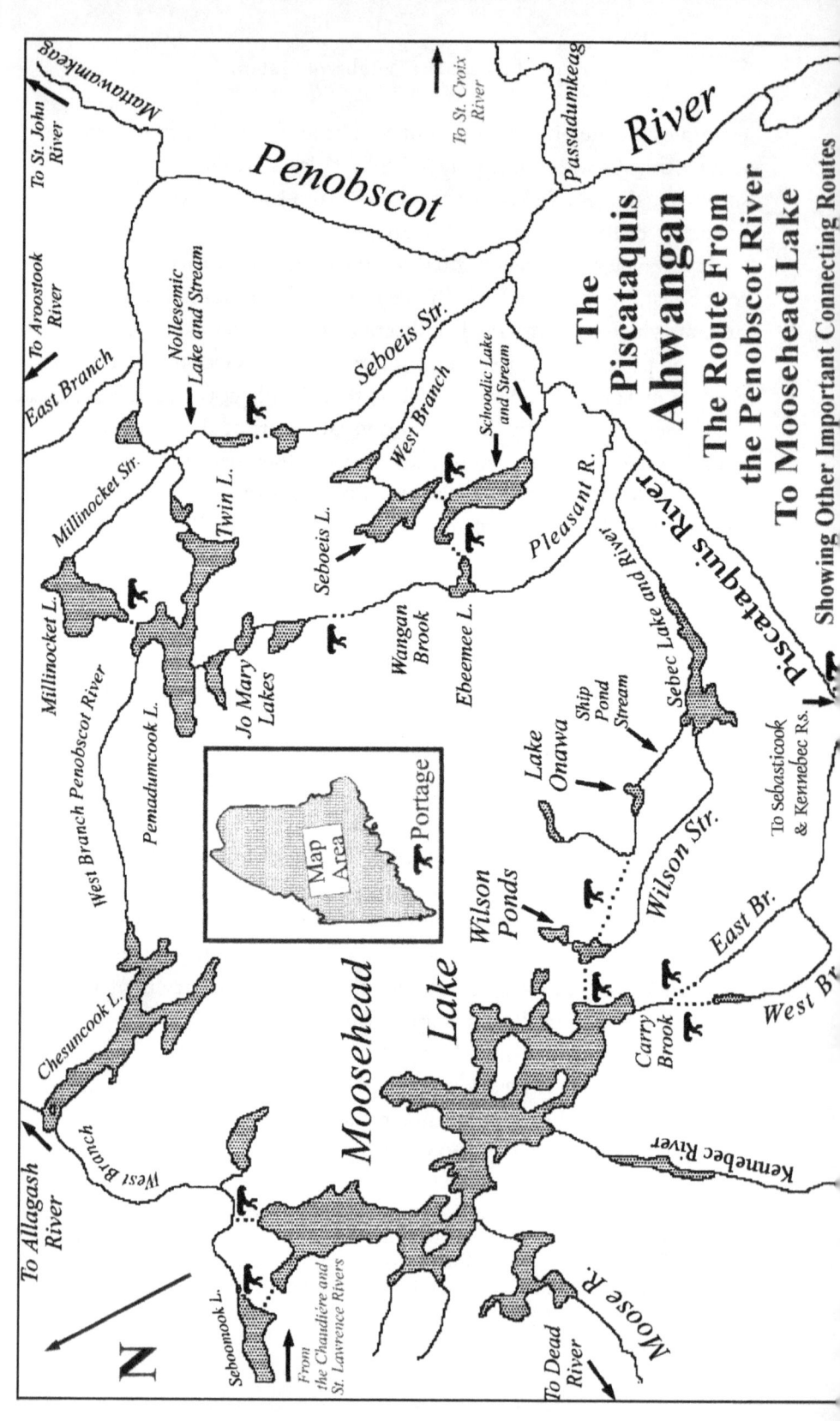

5. The Routes: The Penobscot System

> The Indians are so jealous of their Countery being Exposed by this Survay as made it impractable for ous to preform the work with Acqurice. Altho they waer Ingaged in the service by the Large wages of 3.10 Pr month & Canos %c yet [at Penobscot Island] three of the party Refused to go forward. and the disput between our party & the other Indiens was so graet as to Com to a fray. Which after two days dispute the Result was That I should proced with this Restriction That I should take no Draughts of any Lands but Only wrightings. And saying that when thay waer amongt English Men thay Obayed their Commands & now best way you do Obay Indiens Orders.

After some heated discussion, the Indians agreed to help Chadwick, and he agreed to their demand that he draw no maps. A coalition of eight Penobscot men was hired at good wages. The malcontents watched the more cooperative Penobscots and saw that the survey was done as they demanded.

The party consisted of the following:

John Preble, captain and interpreter, later famous in the Revolution
Joseph Chadwick, "Survayr" and author of the "Journal"
Dr. William Crawford, "2th Survayr," later surgeon, chaplain, justice at Fort Pownall
Philop Nuton (Phillip Newton), assistant

Indian guides:
Joseph Aspequent, "one of your chief sagamores," very sulky and dangerous, according to the colonel at Pownall
Sack Tomah (Jacques Thomas), "an old villain," according to Col. Goldthwait, probably helped Aspequent stir things up
Assong Neptune, "Chief John Neptune, father of the Old Governor" and friendly to whites
Messer Edaweit, a Mitchell, also friendly
Sac Alexies (Jacques Alexis), probably signed various treaties as Alexis or Arexis

Joseph Marey
Sabtes (Jean Baptiste)
Francis
These last three may have been young men.

They came to an agreement early in May, and the four white men and eight Indians set forth on the Penobscot and headed north toward Quebec in four to six birchbark canoes.

Besides surveying the routes between the Sebasticook and Penobscot, Chadwick split his crew into two groups and explored the Piscataquis Ahwangan, the West Branch Penobscot, the North Branch Penobscot, and the major canoe routes into Canada.

After the actual survey was completed, Chadwick drew two or more maps from memory. These maps are good, and along with the map produced by Montresor in 1761, show the major canoe routes between Maine and Quebec.

Chadwick carried correspondence for the Penobscots to Governor Murray in Quebec. The tribe wanted the governor-general to provide them with a "frier free of expense" as the French had always done. The tribe had no "benefit of any techer by which the old men had there Religion the young men could learn non nor have proper Mariages & Christenings &c by all which it was not in there power to live as Christen people ought to do . . ."

The Indians were ultimately disappointed as Governor Murray said he lacked both the jurisdiction and the inclination to do so, not surprising, as he was a Protestant and the Indians were Catholics.

The other part of the correspondence regarded the rights of the Indians to their lands against the encroachments of the white pioneers and contains some insights about Indian life and hints at the reasons for their discontent.

    1764 Indines LANDS so called
sence they had a Conference with Governour Berrnard at Fort Pownall AT which the Indines Ple was. First in the Last War thay ware in an Alience with the French by which thay surposed themsevels to have a Right injoy there Lands in Common with

5. The Routes: The Penobscot System

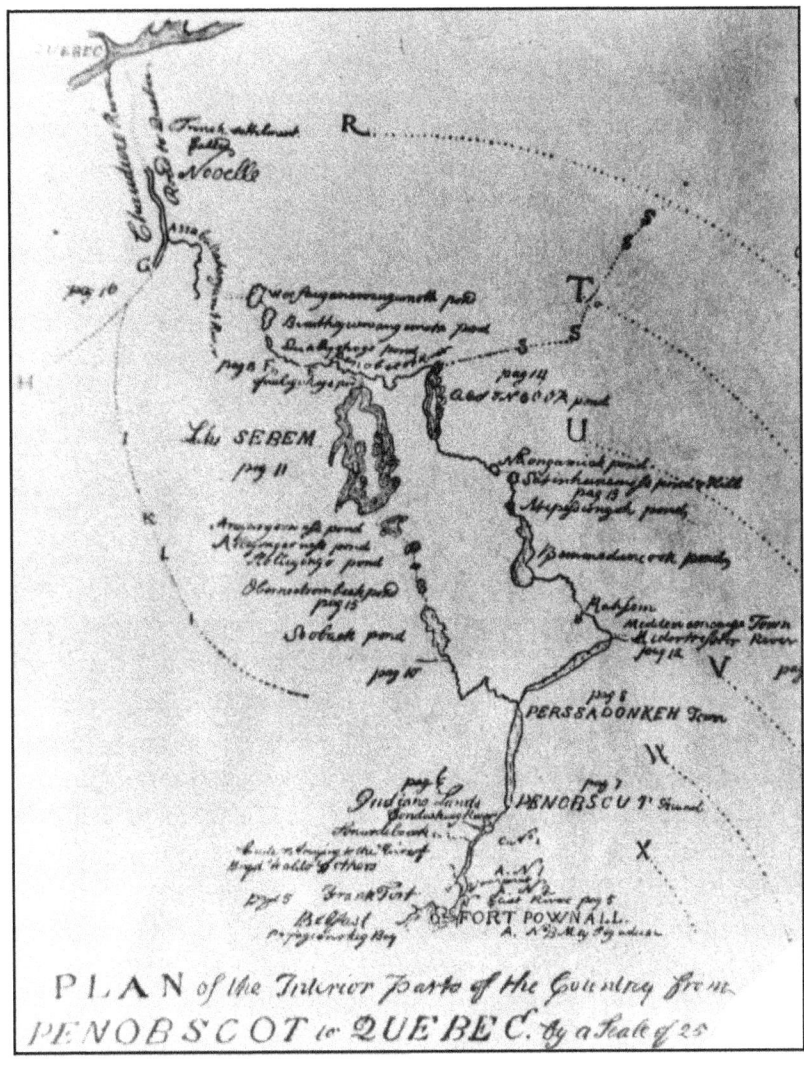

Map by Joseph Chadwick
Sprague's Journal of Maine History, V. 14, 1928

the inhabetence of Cannad by the Capetation That there hunting Ground & Streames ware all paseled out to Certen famelys, time out of mind. That it was there Rule to hunt every third year & kill 2/3 of the Bevier Leving the other third part to breed and that their Beviers ware as much their Stock for a Leving as Englishmens Cattel war his Liveing. That sence the late War

English hunters kill and the Bevier they find on said streames. Which had not only Empovished many Indine famelys but Destroyed the bred of Bevier &c The Governours Answer was that the English should Extend there Settlements above the Falls ... and orderd me to go up & mark out a line and acquaint the people that thay ware not to make any Settlements above the Falls* In Obedence to the above Orders I marked out a Line & acquainted the people & Gave the Indines a Sketch

The reasons that some of the Penobscots were described as "snappish and sullen," or were called "old villain," as was Sack Tomah, can be understood in the context of the message Chadwick was taking to Governor Murray. The over-trapping of the beaver had "Empoverished many Indine famelys" and greatly disrupted their lives.

In the old days, as noted in the dispatch, the Indians practiced conservation of their fur resources, but the English trappers were feeding an insatiable European market and observed no such ecological niceties. The scramble for profit destroyed the "bred of Bevier," and as noted, "&c." The "&c" included the traditional Indian lifestyle. Aspequent and Tomah were unhappy witnesses of their tribe's demise, and they were having a predictable human reaction to such unsettling developments.

To get to Indian Island, Chadwick had ascended a rough section of the river. The four Englishmen portaged past Mat'chi-wis'is, "the bad falls,"[37] over a carry trail that is now buried by Old Town's Main Street. The river falls about seventeen feet in the third of a mile below Old Town and is very rough. The carry trail detoured past this place and put the canoeists back on the river just below the Indian village, Neganodenek, that was, and still is, located on the southern end of the island.

Above these falls the river valley broadens out, and the canoeist finds a large and open river flowing through a flat country of

---

*These falls are Treats Falls, the site of the breached hydropower dam at the modern head of tide at the head of the Bangor Salmon Pool.

meadows and bogs.³⁸ Although Chadwick wrote this 220 years ago, it remains accurate, and it looked like this to him:

> Penobscut or the Ille of penobskeag
>
> The Indine settlements are on the Sutherlynd of an Island [Indian Island] about 1 1/2 Miles in length they have Seven Buildings of about 50 feet in Length & 20 in Breadth Covered with Spruce Bark and Lined with Birch Bark in which are (as they say) 50 famelys Sum remains of the Sells & scrol Iron of a Mass House and one Seevil Gun
>
> The Soil a very yello loum and rokey. Bears Good Indin Corn &c Trees are of a smal growth the Chefe Value of this place is hunting & fishing. At 7 Miles up the River it opens like a Bay Containing sundre Islands and a good Tract of Land about 12 miles in length. The banks of the river about 6 feet hie and appers by the surf to be overflowed in a frishet Soil abov 2 feet depp & appers as a mexture of yallo loum and mud Sum Large roks at about 6 or 8 rods asunder but little or no-Smal Stons bares a Rank jointed Grass & Sundrey Harbs Trees large high Maples Black [modern red] & Gray [white] Oaks Black [yellow] Briches, Littel or no Under brush AT about 4 or 6 furlongs from the River is a good Growth of white pine Tember & Masts & Contenures a level Land to the Mountains which apper blue Note that Mountains do seldom apper blue at a less distance then 10 miles On the Northerly end of this Bay-Lays the Indine Town of Perssadonk
>
> The Land Contenurs a Fertile Soil and a plesant place Good Tember of Sundrey Sorts in perticiler large Gray Oak Trees hear the Indins make Maple Sugar nere Equel to single Retined in Sundre Wiegwoms they have 3 or 400 weight which they say is only a stock for one year in there famelys*

On the west side of Marsh Island, Pushaw Stream enters from the west draining a flat, swampy region marked occasionally by

---

*The effort to boil down this amount of sap, especially with primitive methods, is very hard to imagine.

wandering eskers. This stream is also a route to the Sebasticook and Kennebec waters. An archaeological project conducted by the University of Maine on Pushaw Stream, at "Hirundo and the Young Sites" in West Old Town, has yielded up artifacts which go back seven thousand years.[39]

Above Old Town the Penobscot flows around many beautiful islands, as Chadwick noted. The river is flat for the most part with few substantial falls or pitches and, except when windy, the river is easy canoeing. The current is swift, but the river is shallow enough for poling. There are many good campsites along the river, and many of the old place names give us hints at their history: Sock's Island was named for an Indian baptized by the French as Jacques, but pronounced by the Indians, "Sock"; Sugar Island, for all the sugar maple trees and the Indians' source of sugar; and Mohawk Island,[40] where the Penobscots ambushed and killed a number of Mohawk invaders during the French and Indian Wars. High winds can be dangerous along this part of the Penobscot, because the valley is broad and flat, and whitecaps are common in a high wind. The shape of the valley has the effect of funneling whatever wind there is up or down the river full force. There are few lees to hide behind, although the islands provide some protection. In a strong head wind, the canoeists must go ashore and wait it out, as we do on the larger lakes.

Old Indian village sites occupy the banks of the inflowing tributaries at Olamon Stream, and at the mouths of the Passadumkeag, Piscataquis, and Mattawamkeag rivers. Archaeological work done in this century again seems to indicate an Indian presence of at least seven thousand years thirty-five times longer than the two centuries white people have lived along the banks of the Penobscot.

The Passadumkeag River is one of the most important canoe routes to the east from the Penobscot. The name Passadumkeag means "above the gravel bar," and describes a geographic condition that helped to identify this small waterway for mapless Indian canoe travelers. The name indicates that the route diverges above an obstacle that could not be missed in the main river, a short rapid over a shallow bar and ledge. Strong poling, and a short carry, are

5. The Routes: The Penobscot System

necessary to pass this Penobscot landmark. One-half mile above this place the Passadumkeag flows into the Penobscot River in a rather understated fashion considering its importance.

In the early historic period there was an important Indian village here: Chadwick wrote "that persadonk [the name of the village] may be called one of the most valuable tracts of land," and commercial fishermen still take eels from the Passadumkeag River, as the people that have lived here always have.[41]

From the Penobscot River it is twenty-seven miles to the forks of the Passadumkeag at Pistol Green. The canoeist meets no great obstacles except Grand Falls which must be portaged. The forks are the proper place for the name Nicatowis, "little fork," not the lake above, now called Nicatous (a misspelling of Nicatowis), whose real name in the old times was Kiasobeak, "clear water lake."[42] This was an important spot.

By taking the shorter, right-hand branch of the Passadumkeag, called Nicatous Stream, the canoeist reaches Nicatous Lake and the many canoe routes that radiate from it to all the coastal rivers and territory east to Passamaquoddy Bay.

Kiasobeak, the old name, is found in the name Gassabias Lake, a pond connected to Nicatous Lake by a small and currently alder-choked stream. "Little clear-water lake," something this pond is not, is named after an Indian habit of naming a small pond such as Gassabias as a diminutive of the larger, more important lake.[43]

From Gassabias there is an old three-mile carry to Fourth Machias Lake on the East Branch of the Machias River. Another carry, this one a "long mile," reached Sysladobsis Lake on the St. Croix River system.

South of the route just mentioned, another portage connects to the chain of small ponds, known in the past as the Four Sabaos, which are part of the middle branch of the east-flowing Machias River. Canoes were also carried to the West Branch of the Machias via Campbell Lake.

At the head of Campbell Lake, carries to Eagle Lake at the head of the Narraguagus River and to the West Branch of the Union River passed through difficult terrain.

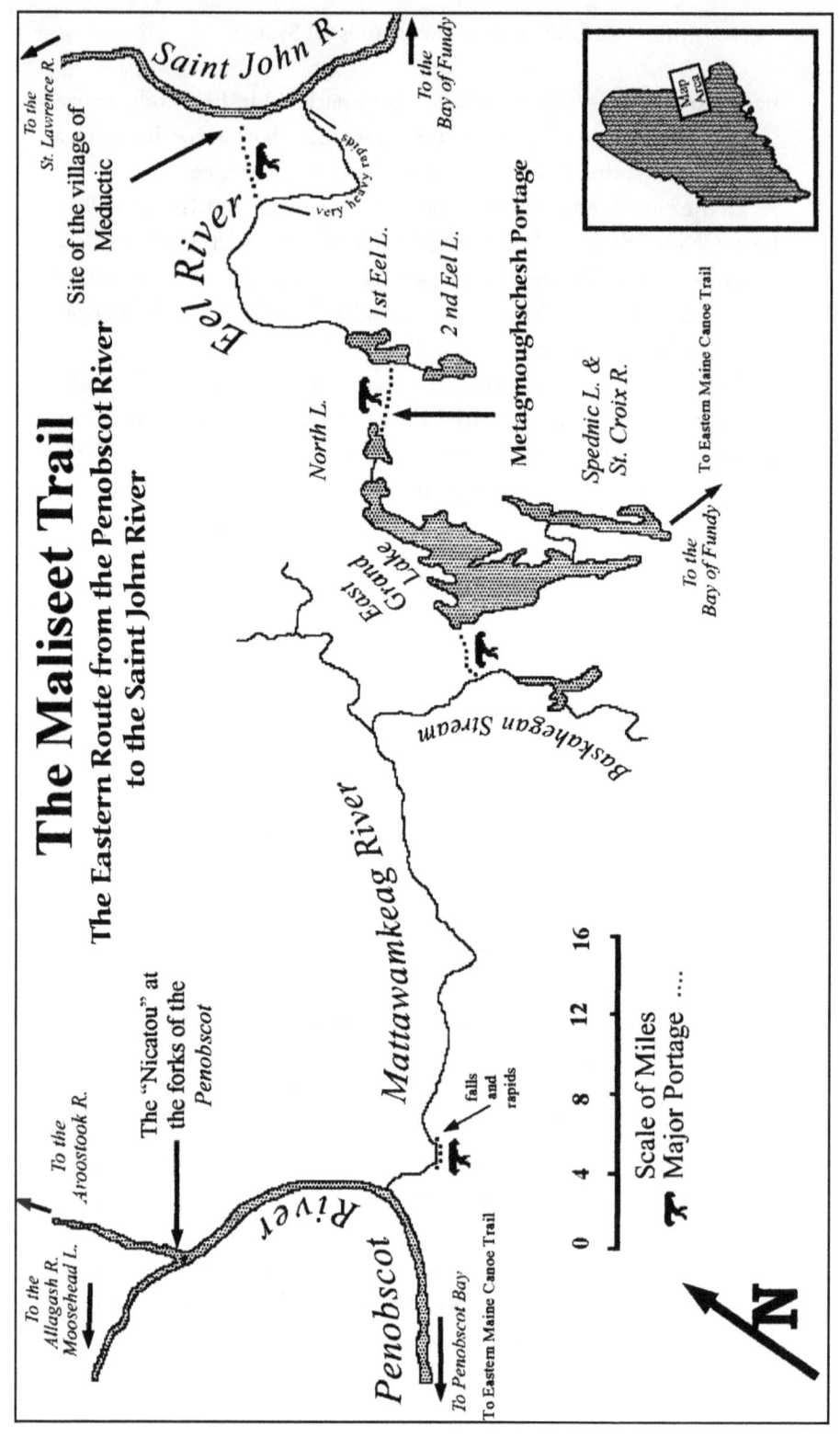

5. The Routes: The Penobscot System

Thus canoe travel was possible to all the important eastern coastal rivers, the lower St. John, and New Brunswick, over the Passadumkeag.

A few miles above the Passadumkeag another very important river, the Piscataquis, "little branch stream," drains the large area south of Moosehead Lake and the land south of the West Branch Penobscot's Lower Lakes watershed.* The Piscataquis flows west to east for eighty miles to its rendezvous with the main Penobscot at Howland, and, along with its tributaries, Seboeis Stream and Pleasant and Sebec rivers, provided canoe routes into the heart of the Maine woods. The Piscataquis Ahwangan was what the Indians called the routes that composed this travel network. For those traveling from the lower Penobscot, or even the lower Kennebec, segments of this network were favorite choices during certain times of the year.

As a route to Moosehead, the Piscataquis and Sebec River approach saved the canoeist over fifty miles when compared to the West Branch approach to Moosehead by Northeast or Northwest carries.

As Joseph Chadwick's party ascended the Piscataquis, he noted that the "Perssacateequees River is mostly a raped Stream & Rockey ruff Land but in some parts are good tracts of land on which grows pine and other tember."

In twenty miles of poling and portaging their canoes and passing the canoe routes up Seboeis Stream and the Pleasant River, the expedition reached the forks of the Piscataquis in modern Milo. Numerous Native American campsites are found all over the region and testify to the long and important role the Piscataquis Ahwangan played in prehistoric Maine. A large prehistoric village site occupies the banks where the Sebec River joins the Piscataquis and has, as have the campgrounds in Old Town and Mattawamkeag, yielded up artifacts seven thousand years old. The arrowheads are made from a type of rock found in New Hampshire, raising the question of their transport.

*The Lower Lakes are North and South Twin, the three Jo-Marys, and Ambajejus, Millinocket, and Pemadumcook lakes.

A smaller campsite, buried six feet deep in alluvial silt, sits atop blue marine clay. Charcoal and flaked quartz material were excavated, and the charcoal has been dated by the carbon-14 technique as ten thousand years old.[44]

Sebec River, only six miles long, is the best canoe stream in this region, with the most dependable flow of water when compared to Seboeis Stream and Pleasant River and also the upper Piscataquis. The Sebec is kept navigable by the water impounded in the large lakes and ponds, Sebec Lake, Onawa Lake, Benson and Long ponds, plus many bogs and swamps that form its headwaters. The Sebec can be canoed when the others are all too "boney" (or very dry) and impassable for birchbark canoes. As a result, the archeological material along the Sebec reflects a heavier use by the ancient canoe people in the number and size of the archaeological sites. The Sebec River route was more widely known than the others and this is shown by the number of exotic (to Maine) lithic materials which are found along the Sebec. I contend that they were brought by birchbark canoe. Chadwick wrote about the region around Sebec Lake. They made their way upriver to "Soback Pond," where the "Land is rockey with eseay asent at sum distance appers to grow hard wood. But the most Valueble Tember is a large furriest of White Cedars many trees are more than 18 inches in diameter & 20 to 30 feet without the aperance of lims."[45]

This beautiful lake, still called Sebec, "a large body of water,"[46] has yielded hundreds of artifacts and again many, as at Moosehead, Sebago, etc., have been lost forever during the last fifty years because of unsystematic collecting.

The route the explorers followed left the head of the lake at Buck's Cove up Ship Pond Stream with a short carry past a small set of falls. In the six miles to Onawa Lake (or as Chadwick called it, Obernecksombeek) canoes can be paddled and poled up a progressively smaller stream for three miles. The last three miles require a portage, either along the stream straight to the pond, or, as Chadwick's party did, northeast into Benson Pond. From Benson the carry is slightly downhill to Onawa Lake. Although a little longer,

5. The Routes: The Penobscot System

this carry route may have offered certain advantages over the more direct route along the stream.

> OBERNECKSOMBEEK Pond has a Vary Remarkable Mounton the which serves to Rectifie our Reckoning about 50 miles Eich way * On the Northerly Sled of this Hill Lays a Good Tract of Land large anouf for a township. Being like Entervale Land the soil is a Brown Loum With sum Sand at 2 or 3 feet depe Trees Large Elems & Maples. On the higher Land Beck & Black Birch trees &C Lays in the Lattetude of 45' 13" and 86 miles computed from Fort Pownall.

Once they had reached Obernecksombeek, they continued up the lake to what is now called the Bodfish Intervale.† There is an old campground here, and Indian artifacts have been plowed up in the fields of the Intervale over the years.[47] The stream becomes too small to canoe just above here, making this place either the beginning or the end of a difficult carry. Shouldering all their wangan, Chadwick's party left the lake and followed the stream up to Long Pond. From there they carried from pond to pond in a westerly direction until they hit Moosehead, Lake Sebem to them, at Beaver Cove.

Some fifty years later, in 1816, Ebenezer Greenleaf (brother of Moses, the mapmaker) led a survey team to Moosehead, but they did not follow Chadwick's route exactly. They came from Sebec up the stream to Onawa Lake, while Chadwick went over to Benson Pond. Once above Onawa, Greenleaf carried directly northwest to Indian Pond, and then to Moosehead, while Chadwick had, more circuitously, gone to Long Pond.[48]

> LAKE SEBEM or Moose Hills
> So called by being Invirond with large Mountin & Rocks, so high as the water Splays up thes rocks are the Coller of Rusty

---

*The "Very Remarkable Mounton," Chadwick's landmark, is Boarstone Mountain, a helpful mark by which to judge progress and direction.
†This place was named for Samuel Bodfish who settled here in 1818.

Iron. & upward a Gray Ston and the tope of the Hills are white all which appers as a fine prospect but the land may be Called waist Land.

Thes parts of the Countrey apper to be the highteth of Land As the Land from the Sea to this place is asending and from thence Descending to the River of St. Larance

From the north end of this Lake by a carrying place* smal pond Sic miles we come into penobscot River."[49]

In traveling north over the Piscataquis Ahwangan, it was customary to ascend the Piscataquis to Moosehead as described. In coming back from Quebec, or from the north, the normal route was down the West Branch to Chesuncook Lake and past Katahdin to reach the main branch of the Penobscot. The current helps the downstream traveler make up in speed and ease what the route lacks in directness.

The Piscataquis Ahwangan was a major travel route during the prehistoric period and most of the archaeological sites show multicultural occupations down through time. Chadwick's Journal does not describe the canoe route above Moosehead Lake, but does describe other important Penobscot places to be discussed later.

Native Americans from the Kennebec often used the Piscataquis Ahwangan. They used the Sebasticook to reach the Piscataquis, then headed up the Piscataquis, following that river to its source in East and West Shirley bogs. From this swamp, a shrunken glacial lake, a short portage into north-flowing Carry Brook connects the Piscataquis with Moosehead and the Kennebec drainage.

For Kennebec Indians to use the Sebec River approach (Chadwick's route) would involve canoeing down the Piscataquis fifteen miles to the Sebec. If the water in the upper Piscataquis was sufficient, the Indians poled it, as it was the most direct route. If the water was low they descended to the Sebec which, as mentioned, maintains a good level of water throughout the summer.

All along the rivers and streams of the Piscataquis system good

---

*This was Northwest Carry.

fishing and camping spots are found, and the availability of food made this network attractive for foraging family groups.

Above the Piscataquis, the Penobscot River remains large with frequent islands and small tributaries until one reaches the Mattawamkeag River, "at the mouth, a gravel bar."[50] This river is the largest of all the Penobscot tributaries and, like the smaller Passadumkeag, was a very important link with the eastern regions of St. Croix and Passamaquoddy Bay, the lower St. John and New Brunswick. The recorded experience of John Gyles, a young captive during the Indian Wars, is the first glimpse we have of the Mattawamkeag canoe route, the interior of Maine, and the way the Indians lived during the early historic period.

John Gyles was eleven years old when he was taken captive by Maliseets during an allied Indian raid on Pemaquid in 1689. Gyles, and others who would prove to be less resilient, were taken in canoes from New Harbor up the coast of Penobscot Bay and Castine's Fort. After a stay of about eight days the Maliseets took Gyles and the others up the Penobscot, ninety miles to the well-known Native American village at Madawamkee (Mattawamkeag). Gyles left no record of this village, but seventy-five years later the "survayr" Chadwick wrote:

> As we pass up the River to this place are many islands which contain many Valuable Tracts of Land & appers to be a plesant place Trees a few large elems & Maples a very rank growth of Grass.
>
> the Shore appers the same But by sum hunters account the Land sune fares into a Spruce Swamp. Mederwomkeag is an Indine Town & a place of residence in time of war but mostly now vacated. In the Mass hous are Sundrey large Books & other things. On the hous hangs a small bell al which the Indiens take care to presarve Land high ground and stony, large tracts of fields & as they say have raised good Indien Corn
>
> The Easterly branch is the Medorwomkeeg in which they pass to Pasemequode & St Johns.

The day after Gyles and his captors reached Mattawamkeag village, they pushed up "the Easterly branch many leagues" to Baskahegan Stream, following the ancient and important route to the St. John. A carry trail spans the two-mile stretch separating the Penobscot from Chiputneticook Lake, headwater of the St. Croix and comes out on the lake at Davenport Cove. Then the route went over to North Lake, upstream from Chiputneticook.

From North Lake the group left the St. Croix system and struggled over the famous and difficult Metagamoughschesh Carry to Eel Lake, which is a headwater pond of the St. John. From Eel Lake they went downstream toward the St. John.

> We arrived at a long carrying place to Medoctec Fort . . . My Indian master went before me [over the carry] and left me with an old Indian and three squaws. The old man said [which was all the English he could speak], "By an' by come to a great town and fort." So I comforted myself in thinking how finely I should be refreshed when I came to the great town.
>
> After some miles of travel we came in sight of a large cornfield and soon after the fort, to my great surprise; for two or three squaws met us, took off my pack, and led me to a large hut or wigwam where thirty or forty Indians were dancing and yelling round five or six poor captives . . . I was whirled among them and we looked at each other with a sorrowful countenance.[51]

Today this site is inundated by the modern hydroelectric dam built downstream. The Meductic Intervale is now flooded, but because of John Gyles, not quite forgotten. Meductic means "at the end of the trail."[52] George Frederick Clark's *Someone Before Us* details his archaeological investigations at the Intervale prior to its inundation a project he fought and the artifacts indicate an Indian presence from Archaic times forward.[53]

The pioneers of Houlton, Maine, also used part of this old route. They came up from the Penobscot by way of Baskahegan to Meductic, the usual way. After making the long and difficult journey to the St. John, they would head north up that river to the junction of the Meduxnekeag.[54] The Meduxnekeag River was an old Indian route from the St. John into the interior of Maine and the settlers followed it and built a town spanning falls that the Indians knew as fishing grounds. There will be more on the Meduxnekeag later.

Gyles was more or less adopted into the tribe and took part in their forest travels. Several years after his capture, he spent a winter with a small band of eight to ten Native American hunters who were equipped with only two firearms. They hunted in the deep interior, three hundred miles up the St. John, "to the northward of the Lady [Notre Dame] Mountains," almost to the St. Lawrence.

Gyles relates that the Indians ascended the river by canoes as far as they could until the winter freeze-up closed the rivers. They continued on foot and made rafts to cross whatever streams or ponds were in their way and were still unfrozen.

When spring came, the hunters made their way back to the St. John headwaters, where they made "bull boats" of moose hides by sewing three or four together and sealing the seams with balsam pitch mixed with charcoal. In these crude craft, they went downriver to a place called Madawescook (Madawaska), and Gyles wrote: "There lived an old man and kept a sort of trading post." At length they arrived at the place where they had hidden their birch canoes in the fall, a long way below Grand Falls.

After their descent of the St. John, the Maliseets planted corn, went fishing, and dug roots to eat "till the corn was fit to weed." After weeding they resumed fishing until the corn was ready to hill. After hilling the corn, they went upriver to take salmon and other fish while the corn ripened. The corn was preserved at harvest by boiling it on the ears "in the milk." The kernels were then scraped from the cob with a clamshell and left to dry on sheets of birch bark. Once dry, the corn was stored in the ground in waterproof "Indian barns" and could be kept indefinitely.

Gyles spent seven years with this tribe and during this time traveled with them from the mouth of the St. John north into the St. John wilderness of modern Maine.

Gyles was redeemed after nine years of captivity and returned to his family.

Baskahegan Stream, "a branch stream,"[55] had other important canoe connections to the coastal regions. Besides the route that Gyles's captors took to reach Chiputneticook and lower St. John, the lower lakes of the St. Croix watershed are accessible from the following Baskahegan portages:

- Tomah Stream which runs into East Grand Lake, a high water route.
- Musquash (Muskrat) River to Big Lake, probably a trapping route to the Schoodic Lakes.
- Scraggly Lake, at the head of the Schoodic Lakes, by a short carry from the Machias River system, and by portage to major routes in all directions.

Above the junction with the Baskahegan Stream, the Mattawamkeag separates into the East and West branches, which parallel each other in a northerly direction and are canoe routes to the east, west, and the north.

From the East Branch, Indians reached the St. John watershed by carrying to the Meduxnekeag, "where the people come out."[56]

Canoeists also pushed up the East Branch as far as possible and made a portage to the north-flowing St. Croix Stream which joins the Aroostook at Masardis.

Both the East and West branches of the Mattawamkeag are very small near their sources, and canoeists need abundant water. During high water the many carries are shorter and the energy-conscious Native people navigated to the highest possible point before beginning their portages. Seasonal water levels were necessarily an important factor for the Indians who canoed these streams.

From the Mattawamkeag's West Branch a larger stream than the East Branch portages went to the East Branch Penobscot.

A few miles above Mattawamkeag are the forks of the Penobscot called by the Indians, Nicatou, "where the route splits."[57] (Remember Nicatowis?) At this point the Penobscot separates into the East and West branches, both major canoe routes and very large rivers.

The East Branch, called Wassategwewick, "place where they spear fish,"[58] is not as long as the West Branch Penobscot but was an important canoe route to the Allagash lakes and Aroostook watershed. This is a very difficult river for canoe travel. It is very swift and has several difficult carries past thundering falls.

An East Branch tributary, Seboeis River, parallels the East Branch and provides an easier access to the Aroostook/St. John country. The Seboeis River is smaller and has a much gentler pitch over its length, although there are difficult and dangerous sections above the modern Grand Lake Road.*

Once travelers reached Grand Lake Seboeis not to be confused with the East Branch's Grand Lake Matagamon the easiest route to the north (or south if coming from the Aroostook) utilized the West Branch of Carry Brook. This branch is connected with La Pomkeag Stream, "rope stream," and the Aroostook, "the beautiful river."[59]

The carry from Coombs Cove on Grand Lake Seboeis to the West Branch of Carry Brook is less than a mile. An alternate route up Wadleigh Deadwater was linked by carry to the East Branch of Carry Brook. This route is through swampy terrain, and the carry is longer and wetter than the West Branch route.

While an ascent of the East Branch Penobscot is difficult, it is by no means impossible. In July of 1979, I canoed down the Seboeis River to the junction with the East Branch, and the water was dropping to the usual summer levels. Upon reaching the East Branch, we (my wife and canoe partner, Meg Cook) turned north and began the difficult push upriver to Matagamon Lake. We were traveling in a ninety-four pound, twenty-foot, cedar/fiberglass Smart canoe. I poled the twenty miles, and we made carries past the sharp falls in one day and a half.

Ascending the Seboeis River requires less effort, but there must be a good head of water. In the low water of summer the larger East Branch Penobscot is easier because the current is not so strong

---

*This road was built in the 1930s as a CCC project from Shin Pond.

then, and the channels are still deep enough to float a canoe. Like other larger rivers, the East Branch is navigable when the Seboeis is too shallow.

Once at Matagamon Lake, the Native American canoe travelers had many options. If they were headed for the Aroostook River or points east, such as the Bay of Chaleur, there were three canoe routes to choose from. They are confirmed by an old map I found in the Maine State Library. In 1813 and then again in 1829, George W. Coffin and Daniel Rose, two explorers, were commissioned by the government to survey the territory between Mars Hill and the western boundary of Maine.[60] At this time the border between the U.S. and Canada was uncertain, and these men were to map a largely unknown territory. On their map, drawn in 1829, Coffin and Rose recorded the various canoe routes that were well known at that time. They obviously traveled by canoe, and the map is most accurate in describing these routes, indicating that they were actually explored.

One route to Millinocket Lake, an Aroostook headwater, from Matagamon utilized Hay Brook, called Nemutchinoetegus Stream by Coffin and Rose. A carry of several miles left the brook and reached the Aroostook drainage above Millinocket Lake.

Another route indicated on their map went up the little East Branch Penobscot above Matagamon (Second Lake) to the Millinocket Portage. A small deadwater brook and a carry of about two miles put the surveyors into Moose Pond at the head of Millinocket Lake.

The third route followed the little East Branch up to its source in Snake Bog, one mile from Haymock Lake, which is part of the chain of headwater Allagash lakes.

In early Indian times beaver undoubtedly constructed numerous dams as they still do on this little-known stream. In 1938 this route was traveled in reverse by Harold Nason and Bill Smith.[61] They came down the Penobscot's West Branch and over the Mud Pond carry to Chamberlain Lake, the traditional Allagash approach. Then, they paddled to Eagle Lake and went east from that lake up Smith Brook to Haymock Lake. Smith Brook was dammed by lumbermen and used to drive logs, although the dam is now gone. After crossing

5. The Routes: The Penobscot System

Haymock Lake, they carried south to Snake Bog and went down the little East Branch. Travel for them was slow as the stream was narrow and rapid in spots. They also had to lift over ten beaver dams in two miles. They reached Matagamon Lake in three days and unknowingly followed the ancient canoe route shown on Coffin and Rose's interesting map of more than one hundred years before.

Coffin and Rose's map indicates that Webster Stream was an old canoe route in the days before the famous Telos Cut of 1842 which connected the Allagash lakes with the Penobscot's East Branch. This rapid stream is followed by modern canoeists from Telos, but few today would ever think of making an ascent to the Allagash or the West Branch Penobscot, although the Indians had done so for many generations. They knew it as Nahmadunkehunk, the "height of land stream."[62]

Included on the Coffin and Rose map are the Native American names of many of these lakes and ponds which, with few exceptions, confirm the names recorded by Thoreau in the 1840s and 1850s and by L. L. Hubbard, who made several trips in the 1880s.

The West Branch of the Penobscot, known as Kettetegwewick, "the main Branch,"[63] was another major route with many options. The Piscataquis River has headwater brooks rising close by the West Branch with relatively short portages to such south-flowing streams as the Seboeis (not to be confused with the East Branch Penobscot Seboeis) and the Pleasant River that show evidence of heavy use by Indian canoeists.

Chadwick scouted the famous West Branch/Moosehead Lake/Kennebec connections over Northeast and Northwest carries. But there is another more obscure and difficult canoe route that connected the Lower Lakes with the great lake the Indians called Sebamook, "a large body of water." To use this route, called Kokadjo-weengwa-sebemsis-ahwangan, the Indians left the western end of Pemadumcook Lake or the West Branch via the Debsconeag Ponds and poled and portaged to Nahmakanta Lake, "where there are plenty of lake trout."[64] From here the travelers followed a carry trail overland to Pollywog Pond, because the stream connecting these two ponds is too steep for canoes.

During the river-driving days of the lumbering era, Pollywog Stream was considered the most difficult and dangerous stream to drive in the Penobscot region,[65] and there are many stories told of river drivers killed along this wild and beautiful brook.*

After the carry into Pollywog, the route continued through Wadleigh Pond, First and Second Musquash ponds into, finally, Penobscot Pond the last Penobscot water on the route. The stream linking these remote ponds is small, and beaver activity is much appreciated by the canoe traveler. In low water this route is most difficult or impossible to use.

From Penobscot Pond a carry trail crossed the divide to the Kennebec drainage and went to Second Roach Pond. From here it was an easy downstream run to Moosehead down Roach River, although this stream can be very shallow in the summer months.

The Kokadjo-weengwa-sebemsis-ahwangan could have been reversed as a connection to the Lower Lakes, as an alternative route to the lower West Branch directly from Moosehead.

Above the Lower Lakes the West Branch flows swiftly through beautiful country in the shadow of Katahdin.

When Chadwick descended the West Branch in 1764, he described Katahdin (which he called Satinhungemoss Hill) as well as the uneasiness of the Native Americans regarding the "highest place." They ascended to the tree line, probably by way of Abol Stream, and Chadwick noted in his own inimitable style:

> "SATINHUNGEMOSS HILL Lays in the Latitude of 45' 43" and from Fort Pownall 184 miles as we traveled and 116 miles by Computation. Bning a remarkable Hill for highteth & figr The Indines say that this Hill is the highest in the Country. That they asend so high as any Greens grow & no higher. That one Indine attempted to go higher but he never returned. The hight of Vegetation is a Horizontal Line about half the perpendiciler hight of the Hill a & intersects the tops of Sundrey other mountines.

---

*The Appalachian Trail traverses this region and could be used to explore this area.

The hight of this Hill was very apperent to us as we had a sight of it at Sundre places Easterly Westerly at 60 or 70 miles Distence It is curious to see Elevated above a rude mass of Rocke large mounting So lofty a Pyramid on which is another rarity. From Above Decends a Stream of water If the observer places himself at such a place that the Rays of Light are Divergine with the falls than the Splay of water as it falls from the hill will appear in as grate a Veriety of Callers as may be Viewd in a Prism glass."

The West Branch is punctuated by sharp rapids with Indian names: Ambajejus, Passamagamet, Debsconeag, Aboljackarmegas, Nesowadnehunk, Ambejackmockamus. Well-worn carries parallel the falls and are still used by canoeists. Upstream, canoeists can pole the channels for many miles, but the river above Nesowadnehunk Deadwater is steep, and a long portage to Ripogenus Lake paralleled the river. To avoid this section from Nesowadnehunk to Ripogenus Lake, especially in high water when the West Branch is dangerous, the Indians used another little-known alternate route.

The Oodoolwagenow-seezicook Ahwangan, or "the Entrails Route," so known for its twisting course, was a detour to, or from, the country above Ripogenus around the dangerous rapids and falls along the main West Branch. This route leaves the West Branch at Nesowadnehunk Stream, "stream that runs between mountains,"[66] with a hard, uphill carry, until reaching the flat terrain at the foot of Katahdin. Here the stream becomes smooth enough to canoe, and the route follows the string of small ponds, Daicey, Kidney, Draper, and Slaughter, all connected by very short carries to Harrington Lake.

Once at Harrington Lake, canoe travelers had several choices. They could follow Ripogenus Stream from Harrington Lake and down into Ripogenus Lake and the southern end of Chesuncook Lake. A short carry west from Harrington Lake connected to Mud Brook and Mud Pond which came out about half way up Chesuncook. By ascending Soper Brook from Harrington Lake and, with another short carry, canoeists connected with Cuxabexis Stream and the upper end of Chesuncook Lake.

This route is hard, especially the first two miles, which required carrying uphill, but the ascent of the West Branch from Nesowadnehunk is also hard. The Entrails Route has short carries and many fine campsites in better hunting territory.

In 1981 the West Branch Archaeological Survey carefully examined the river from the foot of Ripogenus Gorge, at the Big Eddy, to the foot of Big Ambejackmockamus Falls, a distance of four and a half miles. A proposed hydroelectric dam at the foot of "Big A Falls" prompted the exploration which spent three weeks digging hundreds of test pits along the banks of the river at likely camp or portage sites. Hundreds of pits were opened but only two flakes of a chert-like material were discovered. Given the importance of the West Branch, this might seem hard to understand, but can be explained. Native Americans passed through here going downstream and left few campsites above Nesowadnehunk, as there were better campsites below. Canoeists can easily run down through the eleven miles to Nesowadnehunk Falls in about one hour. Those going upriver avoided the place by using the Oodoolwagenow-seezicook Ahwangan.

Ripogenus Dam was built in 1916 and flooded the lakes above Ripogenus into one. Before that, people occasionally found artifacts at Chesuncook, Ripogenus and Caribou lakes, left behind by the Indians. Between the original and much smaller Chesuncook and Ripogenus lakes, there was a half-mile carry that bypassed a steep and rocky gorge separating the lakes. At this spot the channel between Chesuncook and Ripogenus lakes is five hundred feet wide when the flowage is bank full, and it is hard to imagine that there ever was such a gorge. It becomes easier when you stand at the base of Rip Dam, which is ninety-four feet high and holds back millions of cubic feet of water used to generate electricity downriver. Chadwick's description of Chesuncook is difficult to imagine today, given its present, artificial size.

Gesoncook Lake

Very shole water & a mude bottom. In most parts of this Lake our Conoe could not pass within a 100 Rods of the Shore by

5. The Routes: The Penobscot System

which we had not a good View of the Shore and Land. but the Ground appears to be a ded level. Large tracts of Grass Land and at sum distence backwards Riseing with an esey asent Grows a thick Growth of young Trees.

Soil is a brown loum mixt with sum large round Sand but Clear of Stons.

On the Northerly branches of this Lake are Sundre Tracts of Entervale Lands. and upwards in the River for two miles are sundre small Islands all which with the Shore are good tracts of Lands for a Settlement.

Upwards on the River for 20 or 30 miles the Land is broken. Only sum smal tracts of Good Land.

Since the dams have been built, the lake has been substantially enlarged. The erosion caused by the higher water and the action of ice and logs have caused the old soft shores to be eaten away, widening Chesuncook and raising the water many feet in the process. Today the smaller lakes, Ripogenus and Caribou, are merely bays. The "Northerly branches," Chadwick's name for the upper West Branch Penobscot, Caucomgomoc Stream, and Umbazooksus "much meadow"[67] Stream, have also been flowed out for miles above Chesuncook so that they are vastly different. Rapids, falls, and miles of river and stream are now, too, mere bays of Chesuncook.

The West Branch above Chesuncook flows from the region north of Moosehead Lake and south of the St. John and Chaudière headwaters. Carries from the Penobscot River to Moosehead at Northeast and Northwest carries were very important and have already been mentioned. The artificial lake at Seboomook floods the end of the old Northwest Carry along with a twelve-mile section of the West Branch and is called Seboomook Lake, the old name for Moosehead. In low water many artifacts have been picked up along the old riverbank, as well as at the head of the flowage at the forks of the West Branch at Pittston Farm.

This farm was first built in the late nineteenth century to serve the needs of the lumber industry, and later the paper industry, as a farm and depot. At this spot, the West Branch is born by the junction of the North and South branches of the Penobscot. These two smaller streams drain the region along the Maine-Quebec border and both are important links in major canoe routes.

The North Branch rises just to the west of the St. John ponds and is a route to those places and regions to the north downstream on the St. John. To reach Fifth St. John Pond, canoeists poled the eighteen miles upstream from Pittston Farm and then carried over to the pond from Big Bog. Or they carried from Little Bog, upstream from Big Bog, into Sweeney Brook and Baker Lake on the St. John.

These routes were much used by the early twentieth-century guides who took fishing and hunting parties down the St. John. The exact route they chose depended on the water available in the Baker Branch of the St. John. If the water was high, then they went over into Fifth St. John Pond, because Baker Branch is a narrow and rapid eighteen-mile run north into Baker Lake. In midsummer this stream is too shallow to float canoes, and the guides chose to continue up to Little Bog. From here a mile carry connects with Sweeny Brook, a St. John tributary, which drains flatter terrain than Baker Branch and is always full of beaver, the flat-tailed engineers.

Sweeney Brook was used in low water and as the connection *from* the upper St. John *to* the Penobscot. The reason is that Baker Branch is very difficult to ascend as it is a continuous rapid and Sweeny Brook is easier for upstream travel because it is flatter and beaver dammed.

These two streams have been used in this manner for many years by canoeists familiar with the topography. The first river trip Myron Smart helped guide in 1915 utilized this route and, according to Myron's mentor, Louie Nicholas, the Penobscot Indians used Baker Branch as a connection to the St. John by ascending Sweeny Brook when traveling from the opposite direction, back to the Penobscot in the manner I have described.

The South Branch Penobscot is the stream used to gain access to Quebec's rivers and was a very important route.* This stream is also rough in spots and arduous in low water.

---

*The description of the route down from Penobscot Lake is given earlier in the reports of Montresor and Finlay.

These streams served the logging industry for river driving, and all the ponds have been dammed at some time or other. Many of the old "driving dams" have "blown" and hold little water today, but others, like the concrete dam at Canada Falls (which creates Canada Falls Deadwater) is still in place and maintained. Lumbering, river driving, and modern pulp cutting work have had an impact on the cultural material left behind by the Native Americans at many remote wilderness sites. The dam building and log driving has undoubtedly wiped out some of the small and fragile archaeological sites in this region.

The Penobscot was an extremely valuable system to the people who lived by it and to those who traversed its waters to connect with other river systems. There are well-documented canoe routes crossing Maine from the St. Lawrence to the Gulf of Maine and to the east.

Mount Katahdin stands in the center of the Penobscot system, the northern anchor of the Appalachian chain, and was an important landmark for mapless wilderness travelers who used it to rectify their direction. The Katahdinough, the Native American designation for the group of mountains near and including Katahdin, can be seen from many miles away.

The St. John River

The St. John dwarfs all rivers in the region except for the St. Lawrence. This drainage system embraces 21,230 square miles with 7,360 square miles in Maine.[68] As is obvious, this great river had canoe routes from the Gulf of Maine in all directions. The major tributaries that served as important canoe routes in Maine are: the Meduxnekeag River, the Aroostook River, the Fish River, the Allagash, and the upper St. John.

These are the St. John routes into Maine, but this river had many other canoe routes in eastern New Brunswick, north to the Bay of Chaleur and the St. Lawrence that lie outside the province of this work.

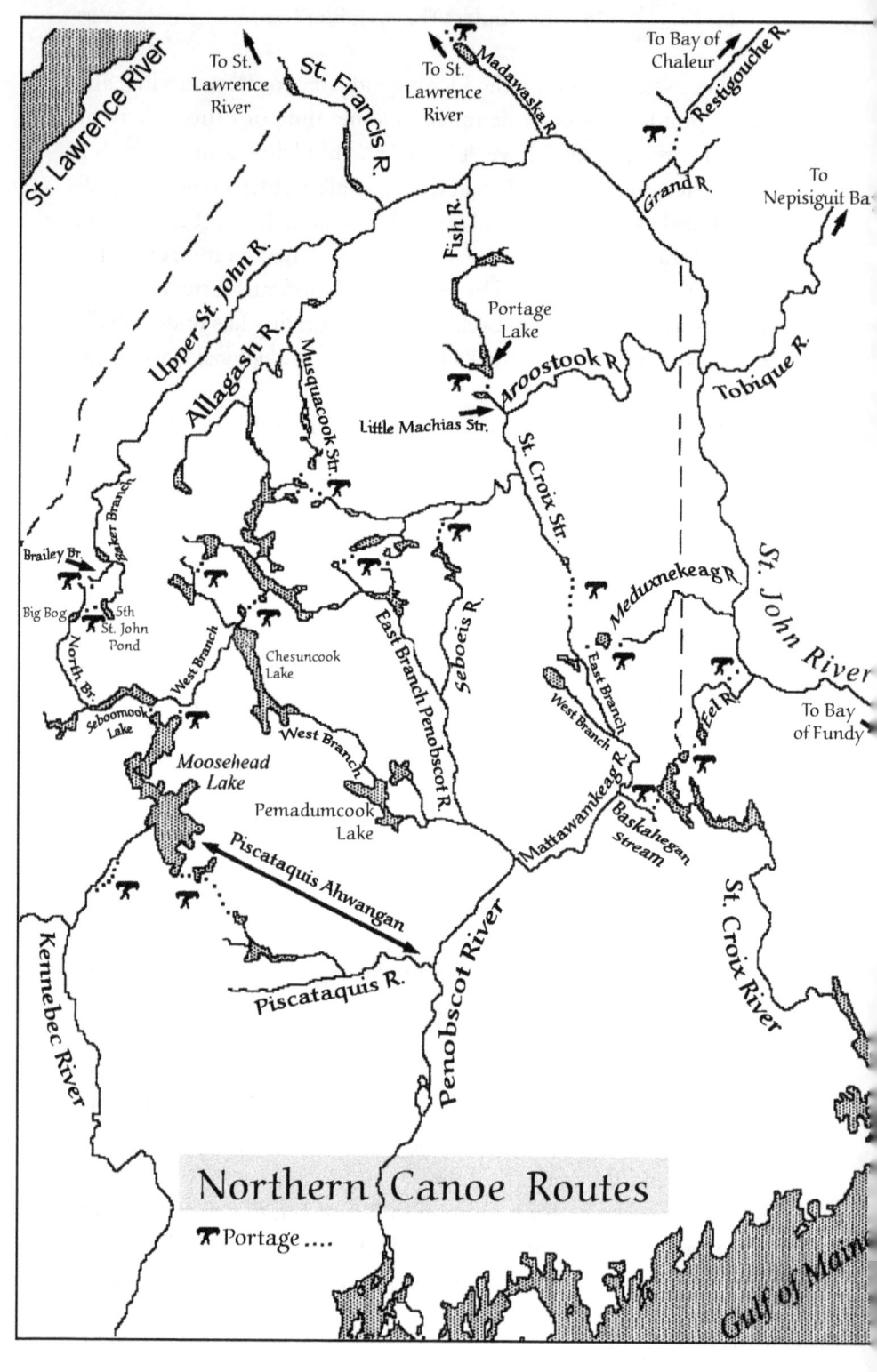

5. The Routes: The St. John River

Some of the St. John's canoe connections with Maine rivers have already been discussed. One, the Chiputneticook/Eel River route, was used by the Maliseets when they made their raids on English coastal settlements. During the Revolutionary War this route was used in one of the most dramatic events that occurred in eastern Maine. The incident involved Col. John Allen and the Maliseets of the lower St. John.

During the war, the British and the Americans both courted the Maliseets as potential allies. The British, stationed on the lower St. John, actively sought an alliance with this tribe, which they hoped would give them political control of that area. The Americans, in the person of Allen, sought to keep them neutral. Allen realized the stakes were control of the eastern wilderness.

Col. Allen denied the British the alliance they wanted by convincing the Maliseets, some five hundred of them, to accompany him and leave the lower St. John for Machias, then under American control.

The route they followed went up the St. John to Meductic and then up the Eel River. They carried over the "Metagamoughschesh portage" into Chiputneticook from which they descended the St. Croix to Grand Falls and the junction with the West Branch of the St. Croix (before it was flooded by dams and when the lakes were much smaller). They ascended this rapid river and made a carry from Big Lake east into the East Machias River, which they descended to the town of the same name.

The tribe left Aukpaque in 128 birchbark canoes. The travelers were troubled by the low water, usual in July, and the problem of feeding such a large number of people. Allen's aide, Lt. Lewis Frederick Delesdernier kept a diary:

July 10. "Our people," including both Indians and those from Port Cumberland, refugees, divided provisions and removed to place of departure.

July 11. "Ambrose, Son and Pierre Benoit set out to pilot our people to Machias."

Sunday, July 13. "At a stream of St. John's river, removed across the carrying place from Meductick, toward the head of Passamaquoddy river, about five miles. It is incredible what difficulties the Indians undergo in this troublesome time, where so many families are obliged to fly with precipitation rather than become friends to the Tyrant of Great Britain, some backing their aged parents, others their maimed and decrepid brethren, the old women leading the young children, mothers carrying their infants, together with great loads of baggage. As to the canoes, the men make it a play to convey them across."

Monday, July 14. "On the stream across Meductick carrying place" We proceeded up the stream four or five miles and stayed this night.

Tuesday, July 15. Proceeded further up the aforesaid stream, over difficult falls, till we arrived at the Pond and went across the same (called Metagmoughschesh) and encamped at the entrance of the portage.

Wednesday, July 16. Carried over Metagmoughschesh portage about four miles, and there encamp, the Indians being much fatigued in carrying canoes and baggage.

Thursday, July 17. Went over a pond (North Pond) and proceeded through a very narrow pass S.W. side of the same it is a carrying place to go co Penobscot River. We went about 7 leagues mostly a south course till we entered the outlet into scoodic River (or rather the lower lake) where we encamped about three days journey from Machias.

From the 18th to 23rd they seem to have sent out hunting parties and parties to gather in the stragglers.

Wednesday, July 23. No provisions in the camp about 1 o'clock crossed a second portage and came into the great lake of Scoodic (More properly the Cheputneticook) have a fine wind to the westward. (Pierre Joe had killed two moose; went ashore and had a great feast.)

Thursday, July 24. Decamp at about 7 o'clock; a fine fresh breeze from the Northward, canoes all under sail, stood the lake. (Found Nicholas Hawas and others who had killed three moose.) "Got out of the lake about six o'clock . . . passed four falls, two of which very dangerous." About sundown encamped.

Friday, July 25. "passed four rapids, then came to a great fall . . . Found moose dress . . . "proceeded and passed four or five very disagreeable rapids and falls, and through several fine lakes.

Monday, 28. "All hands embarked, went down the river and up a branch which they call Pasmagh, stemmed the stream up to the entrance of Passamaquoddy lake (Gena-sor-ga-naw-gum) 127 canoes, all their party.

Wednesday, July 30. Came to a carrying place which appears to be about two miles; came to another carrying place about 12 mile; 3 miles in a small stream; carrying place about 3 miles. Set off down Machias River.

Friday, Aug. 1. Came into a fine lake (Crawford Lake in Crawford).

Saturday, Aug. 2. Reached Machias.

Aug. 8. Indians removed up Coupcheswick, or Western River.

The result of this mass movement was to keep eastern Maine under American control. What a procession they must have made as they came down Grand Lake, over 120 canoes stretched out the whole length of the lake! It must have looked like the modern Allagash River during July and August.

Upstream from the scene of the Maliseet exodus, another stream enters the St. John from the Maine woods, which canoe people have used to connect the big river with several rivers in Maine. The Meduxnekeag River, "where the people come out," branches into several streams, permitting canoe travel in all directions:

- to the south-flowing St. Croix River
- to the Mattawamkeag system over the South Branch Meduxnekeag
- by the main branch to the west into upper Mattawamkeag waters, portages just below modern Smyrna Mills
- and northerly travel to the Aroostook was possible by carry into the Aroostook tributary, the St. Croix Stream, which runs north and joins the Aroostook (and should not be confused with the St. Croix River).

Above the Meduxnekeag, Prestile Stream serves the same purpose though on a smaller scale. Its routes are available during high water and were valuable shortcuts from the Maine woods to or from the main St. John.

The most dependable east-to-west route from the St. John was the Aroostook River. This river served the canoe people in the same way as the other east-west tributaries of major rivers, such as the Sebasticook, Piscataquis, and the Passadumkeag. According to William Francis Ganong, the Aroostook was the most important canoe route from the St. John to the interior of Maine, and the reasons are obvious.

The map of Northern Canoe Routes (page 100) shows that the Aroostook, "the beautiful river," provides direct canoe access to the Allagash lakes and by carry to the Penobscot and regions to the west. This river is of good size and because of the lakes at its head maintains a suitable flow of water longer than the smaller Meduxnekeag or Prestile. Munsungan, Millinocket, Mooseleuk, and Millimagassett streams and lakes provide water and tributary subroutes. Assume that you are about to ascend this beautiful river during a period of "good" (meaning high) water. The following nine options would be open to you.

- **Little Madawaska River** flows south and provides a route to the Fish River lakes via Carry Pond.
- **Presque Isle Stream** flows north and has carries to the Prestile and the Meduxnekeag rivers.

- **Beaver Brook** flows south into the Aroostook and has a carry to the Fish River.
- **Little Machias River** flows south and has a carry to the Fish River at appropriately named Portage Lake.
- **Big Machias River** (sometimes simply referred to as the Machias River, but distinct from the Machias of Washington County) is a sizable stream that flows out of Big Machias Lake and provides access to the route to the cherts of Round Mountain, the Musquacook lakes and Musquacook Stream which drains into the Allagash River.
- **Saint Croix Stream** flows north and provides a canoe route to the Meduxnekeag River, tributary of the St. John, and to the Penobscot's biggest tributary, the Mattawamkeag.
- **La Pomkeag Stream** was a well-known route to the East Branch Penobscot via Seboeis Lake and River.
- **Mooseleuk and Munsungan streams** flow southeast and provide routes to the Musquacook and Allagash lakes and the Penobscot's West Branch.
- **Millinocket Stream** is a headwater stream of the Aroostook River and has carries to the East Branch Penobscot and Allagash lakes.

The Aroostook was important for more reasons than its many canoe routes. As mentioned above, the Aroostook rises very close to important outcroppings of rock, called "Munsungan cherts," that the Indians needed as raw material in weapon and tool manufacture.

These Munsungan cherts, like the felsite of Mount Kineo, have acted as a magnet drawing people into the Munsungan Lake region since the end of the last Ice Age, twelve thousand years ago. At some point they began coming by canoe. A careful study of the canoe routes and the incidence of Munsungan chert in archaeological collections may hold some important insights.

During the 1970s the Center for the Study of the First Americans (CSFA) conducted a four-year multidisciplinary archaeological study of the Munsungan region which proved that human beings visited the outcroppings of cherts at Norway Bluff and nearby Round Mountain eleven thousand years ago and left behind the characteristic Clovis-style "fluted points," the oldest projectile point type known in North America.

Subsequent Native American cultures also utilized the cherts of Norway Bluff and Round Mountain, and their artifacts abound in archaeological sites throughout the Northeast. The Munsungan Project has uncovered the 11,000-year evolution of local stone tool technology which may give us important information about the age of the canoe and the patterns of trade and travel the Indians developed over time.

A limited study conducted on the distribution of the Munsungan cherts over the Penobscot watershed indicates that the chert that was carried the longest distances was of the very finest quality. All of the chert artifacts from Penobscot Bay are of the "Christmas tree" variety, so named by the Munsungan archaeologists for its characteristic red and green colors.[69]

Closer to the source of the cherts, at Grand Lake Matagamon, on the East Branch Penobscot, artifacts have been found that are of much coarser Munsungan material. It stands to reason that people who either traveled all the way to Munsungan to get the cherts, or traded something valuable for them, would want to get the best materials their fur and other trade items would buy.

The Aroostook River finishes its eastern run entering the St. John almost across from the mouth of the Tobique River, an important canoe route through New Brunswick to the Bay of Chaleur. As one ascends the main St. John, several important river routes were available to the Gulf of St. Lawrence, or to other New Brunswick river routes.

The main St. John River is very close to the Fish River system, and there were several connections. The Fish River contains nine good-sized lakes strung out in a northeast to southwest direction and connected by the Fish River, which joins the St. John at Fort Kent. Canoeists did not ascend the main St. John to Fort Kent to reach these lakes. As noted in the description of the Aroostook, the Fish River was readily approachable from several tributaries of the

Aroostook (Little Madawaska River, Beaver Brook, Little Machias, and Big Machias).

The name Portage Lake memorializes the old connection from that lake over to Aroostook waters. Cross Lake refers to the fact that the canoeist would cross this lake. Carry Pond, the name speaks for itself, part of the Aroostook system, is located just to the east of Cross Lake and drains into Madawaska Lake, which runs into the Aroostook. Like other places in canoe country, the Indian place names, Carry Pond, Meduxnekeag, and Portage, provide clues that help us learn about the people who named them in the first place.

Besides the Aroostook River canoe routes to the Fish River system, the other routes went from the main St. John River over small brooks and short portage trails. Ganong reports the existence of these routes in a general map but without much detail. The regions just east and north of the lakes are drained by Violette and Thibodeau brooks. Travelers from the St. John carried from the river and entered the "back door" of the Fish River which is a short route through the interior and has connections with more important points.

The Fish River is easy to ascend by canoe and, because of the big lakes, maintains a dependable flow of water. In a dry season the best way to the Fish River would be directly from the St. John by carry over into Long Lake, or up the Fish River. Many of the Aroostook tributary routes become very dry and impossible for canoeing in mid to late summer, unless sufficient rain falls to keep the streams full.

There are interesting subroutes within the Fish River system that are created by the lay of the streams and lakes. First, there is "the Carry," a path of less than one mile that connects the eastern end of Eagle Lake with Square Lake. A portage between these lakes would save a long paddle and would be useful in bad weather.

The Red River is a direct route southwest from St. Froid Lake to Fish River Lake. Three lakes, St. Froid, Portage, and Fish River Lake, make a triangle. By using Red River to reach Fish River Lake, a canoe traveler goes directly there on one leg of the triangle. The Red River flows directly from the Fish River Lake area and saves many miles of upstream canoeing. The difficulty of the short portage between the lake and the Red River is quicker and much less taxing than the long upstream push south and then northeast to Fish River Lake over two legs of the triangle.

Canoeists have the customary flexibility for coming downriver from the lake, as they could use the Red River route, or follow the Fish River downstream through good hunting and fishing country.

These routes were well known by the early guides and explorers of the Maine woods. One good account of this route one hundred years ago is T. S. Steele's *Paddle and Portage,* which describes canoe trips taken in the 1880s. Steele's party approached the Aroostook from Spider Lake on the Allagash via the old, and now overgrown, Osgood Carry. This route is impassable today because the brook above Spider Lake is obstructed for miles with brush from pulp-cutting operations. Steele's party encountered low water, since it was late in the fall. Upon making the portage into Echo Lake, they found the outlet stream too low to float their loaded canoes. The enterprising guides rebuilt an old beaver dam at the foot of the lake, and after a day and rainy night, they had stored enough water to allow them to wade their canoes down steep Chase Brook to the lake of the same name above Munsungan Lake. Below these lakes the river is deeper, but they still had to make protective cedar "shoes" for their canoes. One of Steele's guides split out some cedar slats which were then lashed to the hull. These shoes lessened the chance of damaging the canoes which they towed in shallow water.

In 1881 Lucius L. Hubbard wrote in his well-known *The Woods and Lakes of Maine* that he had been caught by similar conditions and an early freeze up in the Musquacook lakes. Hubbard's trip began at Moosehead and was bound for New Brunswick. He came by way of the West Branch Penobscot and across the Mud Pond Carry into Chamberlain Lake. They carried over into the Musquacooks from Pleasant Lake. They too had to "shoe" their canoes and wade them downstream.

Fortunately both Steele and Hubbard had guides well drilled in the ancient canoe travel strategies.

Many old campsites used first by the Native people and followed by the explorers, lumbermen, and tourists are still in use throughout the Aroostook watershed. Along the lower reaches, many have been located by local residents while plowing their fields on the fertile flood plains or "flats" of the river. Many of these potato-field sites are on fossil river channels, sometimes one hundred yards from the current riverbank. The river has changed its course in the time since humans first came to the region, and some of the artifacts found near Ashland indicate a human presence going back nine thousand years. Most of the material is Munsungan chert with some quartz artifacts as well.

The Allagash

In describing the Allagash and upper St. John canoe routes we will have come full circle in a geographic sense. These two large north-flowing rivers run from the same headwater plateau that spawns all the other big Maine rivers.

The Allagash is a wonderful canoe river. While there are rough sections and long carries, the Allagash is much easier to ascend and has more dependable water levels than does its longer twin, the upper St. John. About fifty of the one hundred miles of the Allagash are made up of lakes which can be paddled at any time of the year except in winter. Today the lakes are larger than they were in prehistoric times because of the dams, but there have always been lakes and deadwaters along the Allagash that made it a good canoe route.

From the main St. John River, at the Allagash village, canoeists have to pole the first section of the Allagash to Round Pond. The river is good poling, however; the bottom is gravelly and provides a good pole hold. The irregular banks and numerous islands provide eddies that are a great help when going upriver. Some of the rapids, like those of Twin Brook Falls at the end of the modern Allagash Wilderness Waterway, require a short carry, as do Allagash Falls seven and one-half miles upstream.

Musquacook Stream enters the Allagash at Musquacook

Deadwater and drains a series of small ponds that lie roughly parallel with the course of the Allagash. This stream, and its string of ponds, provides an alternative canoe route up or down the Allagash when the water is high enough. The rapids on the smaller Musquacook are easier to pole through than those on the Allagash and are more protected from the elements than the larger, more open river. Musquacook means "birch-bark place," and some place along the stream was evidently a source of this valuable material used for canoes, houses, and many other practical objects.[70]

Another side route that parallels the Allagash on the west is found over Chemquasabamticook Stream up the lake of the same long name, which means "stream that runs from the mountains."[71] The hills are those to the west of the Allagash, and this stream is an excellent high-water route. Today the Indians of the Allagash have abbreviated the name and call it Sebemsicook Stream and Lake. From this lake one may carry through the woods about two miles over to Thoroughfare Brook and descend that stream to the junction with the main river at the head of Churchill Lake. This small brook is plugged up by beaver and is easy to follow.

Chemquasabamticook Lake is connected with tiny Allagash Pond many miles above Allagash and Chamberlain lakes. The Allagash headwaters rise very close to the southern shore of Chemquasabamticook Lake, and canoeists can use upper Allagash Stream to penetrate the interior region between the Allagash and the St. John. This stream may also have been used as a connecting link between the Allagash and St. John. A slightly longer carry to the west of the Allagash connects with the St. John brooks which run into the main river below Baker Lake.

The old name for Priestly Lake is Awanganis, "the little route."[72] This lake and its outlet Drake Brook provide a protected out-of-way canoe route that lies close to Allagash River and flows through hunting and trapping territory.

One of the major Allagash canoeing obstacles for those headed upriver is Chase's Rips. These rapids are today controlled by the dam at Churchill Lake, which releases water on a regular basis during the summer to flush downriver the thousands of canoeists who travel the Allagash Wilderness Waterway every year. When the gate is open and the water is running strong, the rapids resemble the Horserace on the West Branch Penobscot below Big Ambejackmockamus Falls. The waves are large and the water is deep which makes the poling very hard. The pole vibrates back and forth, quivering in the hand, as the swift water sweeps past. When this vibration becomes severe, usually when poling in water four to six feet in depth, it is time to get out of the canoe and carry until the current eases up.

Downstream canoeists easily run the whole nine miles of Chase's Rips, but the upstream voyager has to carry the severest sections while poling the rest.

At Churchill Lake the deadwater paddling begins, with the only danger and it is considerable being the wind. Canoeists are frequently stranded for days along these shores of the big lakes while they wait for the winds to abate. The lakes and the prevailing winds both head north-south, and whenever the wind is blowing the long exposed stretches are whipped up into whitecaps and large waves. Many canoes have been, and will be, swamped on these lakes, and fatalities are quite common.

Many important canoe routes diverge from the Allagash lakes. The connections with the Penobscot watershed have already been discussed, as has the Allagash/Aroostook connection. But there are others that exist and may have been important.

One intriguing example is the route from Chamberlain Lake to Allagash Lake via Ellis Brook and its several deadwaters. This small stream rises in Ellis Pond, about one mile from the southern end of Allagash Lake. The terrain is flat, and the stream is impounded by the beaver. At the mouth of Ellis Brook on Chamberlain Lake, there is a set of sharp rapids that is a good fishing and camping spot. Trout abound at this spot, and it has been well known to guides for many years. Ellis Pond and Brook can also be reached from Little Shallow Lake, one of the Penobscot ponds connected to Caucomgomoc Lake by Ciss Stream. The advantage of this route is its direct line from the middle of Chamberlain to Allagash Lake.

The Allagash interlocks with its own tributaries and the neighboring rivers in such a way that it was of major importance to the Native Americans. At the time of European arrival, the northern interior evidently did not support a permanent indigenous Indian population but was a general hunting/trapping territory, a sort of no-man's land.

The Upper St. John

The St. John's upper and longest tributary, the Southwest Branch, flows southward over 130 miles from the cluster of St. John ponds. The small stream is the Maine-Quebec Border for many miles and can be reached from the upper Penobscot region.

The upper St. John valley is quite large and shallow, so high winds can hamper the canoeist. Downstream travel is swift and easy, but upstream canoeing is difficult. The rapids are fairly shallow drops over gravel banks devoid of the large rocks and their helpful eddies. The eddies behind the irregularities of the shore or islands are often too shallow for canoes, which have to be tiringly held in the relentless current most of the time.

In mid to late summer this section of the St. John is usually too shallow for canoes. The upper St. John, unlike the Allagash or Penobscot, has no headwater lakes to contain its seasonal precipitation. The result is, when the spring runoff is over, so is the canoeing on the upper St. John. During such times, the Allagash, however, maintains a navigable flow.

Several of the St. John's tributaries flow from Quebec in the west. The St. Francis River, Little Black River, Chimenticook Stream, Big Black River, and the Daaquam River are canoe routes to and from the St. Lawrence valley. Ganong has reported that these routes were much used by the French Recollets and the Jesuits in the 1630s and 1640s, as they went back and forth between Quebec and their tribal missions in Maine and the Maritimes.

Little archaeological material has been located along the upper St. John River, save for sites at the mouth of Big Black River and a few others. This area was explored during the preliminary studies of the Dickey-Lincoln Hydroelectric Dam Project, and little was found supporting the assumption that this area was sparsely settled by the Native Americans.

One factor in this is the extreme fluctuation of the water levels during the year. Erosion and the damage of ice and log drives during the spring flood have hastened archaeological destruction along the low banks of the St. John. Another factor is the relative lack of attractiveness of the upper St. John when compared to the Allagash. If it was used mostly for downstream travel during high water, the archaeological sites would be more widely distributed than those along a river which was used for travel in both directions.

With this we come to the end of the outline of the canoe routes of Maine. We can still follow most of these old routes, but often the smaller links are so clogged with debris that they cannot be used. They all can be easily explored by using canoe in conjunction with a car or pickup truck.

The paper-company roads cross or parallel many remote streams and ponds that once were important links in the canoe route network. Today the best way to explore these spots is to drive as close as possible and then put the canoe in the water, if that is possible. Some of the headwater streams are still open to the canoe, but just as often brush or low-water conditions make canoeing out of the question. Even during the spring flood, many of these small and now unused thoroughfares may be too clogged to allow canoes to pass.

Chapter Six

The Canoe Routes Today

What are the canoe routes like today? Some of what has just been said will provide insights, especially for those who have little familiarity with canoes. Along the lower reaches of our major rivers, where most of the modern human population lives, the rivers have been harnessed for hydroelectric power generation. Many of the rapid sections are now submerged behind large dams; churning falls and pitches no longer waste their energy in a noisy roar and mist. On the Androscoggin, Kennebec, Penobscot, to name just the biggest rivers, these places are now quiet except for the hum of electricity. Archaeological sites abound at such places and all have not been wiped out by major construction activities. There is a major Indian campground/portage trail near the Caratunk Falls Dam on the Kennebec, which has survived several dams, which remains to be analyzed.

Industry and agricultural activity, however, have claimed many sites along the riverbanks. Early farmers often plowed up Indian artifacts in flood plains and on riverside terraces, and many private citizens and local historical societies have cabinets full of such finds.

Industrial activity has not been limited to the southern portions of Maine, and some of the most remote spots today are littered with the rusty debris of the Industrial Revolution. Modern technology has increased the rate of obsolescence, and scattered in the path of the lumberman and paper maker is an incredible array of junk, an endowment to future generations of archaeologists. The Indians evidently required thousands of years to develop a new projectile point style or gouge, and they left few of them lying around.

6. The Canoe Routes Today

One way to understand some of the manmade changes along the old canoe routes is to examine one place that used to be important but is forgotten today. I am speaking about the Mud Pond Carry.

The Mud Pond Carry was important because it is where the Penobscot and Allagash rivers come within two miles of each other, and the carry was the easiest and shortest route between them.

From Umbazooksus, the "much meadow" stream, on the Penobscot side of the carry, the trail goes over a barely perceptible height of land to Megkwakagarnik, or "Mud Pond," according to Lucius L. Hubbard. This small and unprepossessing pond drains into Chamberlain Lake which received its modern name when, in about 1850, a young hunter drowned there. He had come from The Forks of the Kennebec to hunt moose with his father and friends and upset a canoe. Hubbard tells us the Indians called Chamberlain Apmoo'gene gamook, "the lake that is crossed," in reference to the several canoe routes that do just that.

The first record of the carry was left by Maine's first "out-of-stater," Henry David Thoreau. The man from Walden came to Maine

three times to explore, see moose, and learn about Indians, and in 1850 he passed over the Mud Pond Carry to explore Chamberlain and the East Branch Penobscot. The carry was occupied by a squatter named Jules Thurlotte who earned a meager living lugging other people's wangan back and forth over the trail on his back. Thoreau didn't visit there but noted:

> Our path ran close by the door of a log hut in a clearing at this end of the carry, which the Indian who alone entered it, found to be occupied by a Canadian and his family, and that the man had been blind for a year . . . This was the first house above Chesuncook, and the last on Penobscot waters and was built here, no doubt, because it was the route of the lumberers in the winter and the spring.

The exertions of being a "toter" had caused poor Thurlotte's physical decline and blindness, but before he lost his health, Thurlotte established the all-time lugging record for the Mud Pond Carry when he carried a hogshead of salt pork with the brine drained off across to Mud Pond.

Thoreau continued:

> After a slight ascent from the lake through the springy soil of the Canadian's clearing, we entered on a level and very wet and rocky path through the universal dense evergreen forest, a loosely paved gutter merely, where we went leaping from rock to rock and from side to side, in the vain attempt to keep out of the water and mud.

In 1859 Thurlotte's wife abandoned him on the carry and ran off with a hunter named Joe Goodblood. She also left two "Baby Girls Thurlotte" buried at Chesuncook Village.

After Thurlotte, the carry was "operated" for a time by Ansel Smith, the pioneer of Chesuncook Village. In 1880 Ansel Smith, Jr. brought the first team of oxen to work on the carry, and in 1926 he recalled "that there was hardly a path there then and so thick was the growth of the forest that one had to bend low and push the bushes to either side in order to get to the lake." He maintained a small camp at the west end of the carry and told Lucius Hubbard in 1883 that he expected to make $120 toting that season.

Another Smith brother, Frank, took over the carry business in 1891 and built a large log camp on the Umbazooksus side and widened the clearing.

In 1902 Howard Colby, a New Jersey sport and frequent visitor at Moosehead's famous Kineo House, bought Smith out. He placed Ed Ranco in charge of the toting and built a set of sporting camps and opened up a four-acre clearing. In 1916 Ranco himself bought the camps and business and worked there for the next twenty-four years. He hired one man to canoe the mail back and forth over the twenty-six miles of the West Branch to Northeast Carry, and he also hired a teacher to educate his children.

The sleds and wagons that the toters used cut into the soft soil and made the trail like a straight brook. I have waded my canoe up the trail when, after a hurricane, the water was very high, and the woods were soaked by several inches of rain; I had mistaken it for a brook.

In the 1920s the Chesuncook, Chamberlain and Eagle Lake Railroad was constructed to haul wood from the St. John watershed to the Penobscot, and the right of way intersects with the carry trail about one hundred yards from the old campsite. While the trains have long since shut down and now quietly rust on the shore of Eagle Lake, pickup trucks and campers kick up the dust occasionally. The last toter, Frank Cowan, gave up in 1957. Since then canoeists have had to carry their own gear.

The result of all of this activity has probably devastated whatever the Indians left behind over the centuries. The carry trail is impossible to lose as Thoreau did in 1857. In 1977, a very wet year, I explored the Mud Pond Carry. The trail was marked by a forked stick with a birchbark sign advertising CARRY TRAIL, and a black plastic garbage bag, knotted onto an alder, fluttered glumly in the breeze beside the sign. The clearing has grown up to alders which stood out against the orange of the budworm-infested spruce-fir forest, and a short search revealed the litter of the last one hundred years. Bottles, cans, wagon wheels, and even telephone wire mark the place. I didn't find the Monson slate fireplace hearths that Colby brought in. Someone must have carted them off. Perhaps the ghost of Jules Thurlotte is still a-toting.

The trail is still wet and the forest thick as Thoreau has told us, but the marks of modernity can't be missed. It will be many years before the scars of the last hundred years vanish. Many of the other carries in Maine were used by the lumbermen for the same reason that the Indians used them and may have had their archaeological records disturbed, if not destroyed.

The routes have changed and so have the people who travel in canoes. I enjoy the folks I meet on canoe trips, for the most part. The skilled guides, recreational paddlers "getting away from it all," and fishermen one meets often add to the pleasant memories of a canoe trip. Occasionally one meets wide-eyed thrill seekers, armed with a certain zest, but innocent of any knowledge of canoes, Maine camping techniques, or woods etiquette. Such people *Ignoramus americanus,* a species of human unknown in the deep woods of Maine until the modern roads were built usually lack maps but come equipped with battery-powered radios, plenty of beer, and sometimes, especially around the Fourth of July, firecrackers.

I have spent more than one night camped beside such parties and would have gladly traded them for a lonesome black bear foraging for garbage or some other handout. While bears can be frightening, they can be chased off with a flashlight and a couple of well-aimed rocks, not so with *Ignoramus*. The only cure for them is strong paddling the next morning.

I recently ran into such an outfit on the Allagash at Churchill Lake and found them amusing to a point. I do not bemoan the fact that the woods and rivers are now open to virtually everyone I like that but I do bemoan the attitudes that this group expressed with the dirty campsites they left behind, the lack of care or understanding of what they were about, and the lack of respect for their equipment or the people they encountered.

We first met them at the carry at Churchill Dam while we waited for the Allagash Waterway warden to haul our wangan past the rough section of Chase's Rapids, the roughest section on the river. The wardens provide the service, and we decided to have our gear hauled downriver by truck several miles, so we could run the rapids in empty canoes and avoid soaking our stuff in the standing waves found along that section. We had just gotten dried out after several wet days and nights and didn't want to chance another soak, so we sat in the sun below the dam awaiting the return of the warden. Our canoes, an eighteen-foot Old Town Tripper, and my twenty-foot Smart River Queen, were tied up to the bushes on the shore, as we rested and talked.

As we sat there enjoying the warmth of the day and the roar of the river, a strange-looking group filed down the path, six men and four women. One of the women approached and asked, "Have any of yuhs ever done this before?"

The men, attired in camouflage jungle fatigue pants, stood back, too macho to ask about anything. I did notice some concern on their faces. The roar of the Allagash below the dam had scared some members of this group. This fear was healthy and was about the only sign of intelligence that one could detect.

"None of us have ever done this before," the woman went on, and she related, nervously, that they had decided to "do the Allagash," while barhopping in Boston, their hometown. They could have come from anywhere even the state of Maine, I'm afraid.

They had five canoes, all rented, and only one, a seventeen-foot Old Town, was suitable for such an Allagash trip. The other four canoes were made of aluminum, fourteen feet long, and narrow. Their paddles were made of hollow yellow plastic and were about three feet long. I noticed them looking at our big canoes and long hardwood Smart "power-puller" paddles and then glancing at their stuff. For them this was the first rough water on the trip, and they began to get the idea that this could be dangerous.

The men became more talkative and we chatted for a few minutes. Two of the women refused to run the rapids and decided that the warden would haul them along with the gear; the others decided to "go for it." They had become excited about the run ahead of them and started to challenge each other as to who dared to do what with loud talk and epithets.

The warden returned and we put our stuff along with theirs into the warden's pickup and headed downriver with the Bostonians bringing up the rear.

We shot the rapids easily. Our empty canoes rode high upon the waves, and except for hearing an occasional holler or the crunch of aluminum on a rock and sighting a head or two bobbing in the foam, we saw little of the Bostonians until we reached the bridge.

We pulled our canoes into the eddy below the bridge and met Gil Gilpatrick, a well-known guide, canoe builder and author, and his wife. Gil was on the river taking pictures for his book, *The Allagash*, and we talked with the two of them while we awaited the arrival of our gear. It was a hot and sunny day, and we decided to eat our lunch there while we waited. The sky was a deep blue, and big white clouds were being driven by a wind out of the northwest, a portent of good weather.

Soon the Bostonians would hove into view. They were, except for the two girls in the seventeen-footer, soaked from several swampings but, as they wore their lifejackets, none the worse for wear. The girls had simply kept their canoe headed downriver, and as it was bigger and more seaworthy than the men's aluminum canoes, they had made the four-mile run safely, only shipping several inches of water.

The oldest man, about thirty, seemingly made more friendly by the excitement, sloshed over to us, asking solicitous questions about how we had fared in the rapids, followed quickly by an attempt to bum a cigarette. When he found out we didn't smoke, he became much less talkative and amused himself sorting out his soaked smokes, hoping against hope to find a dry one. The other canoes in his party were still behind, as the paddlers had stopped to dump the water out.

When the girls in the Old Town came into view, he stood up on the bridge and hollered (all in one sentence), "Hey, Debbie, how did yuhs make it yuh got any cigarettes?"

While Debbie and her partner had successfully negotiated Chase's

Rapids, her smokes, floating in four inches of water, had not been so lucky. When the alpha male got the shouted reply about the soggy cigs, he turned away with a muttered "s——" and glumly sat back down to await the warden.

He, and the others, did something that we found exceedingly strange at this point. They had beached their canoes *above* the bridge rather than pulling into the gentle eddy below. The upstream side of the bridge is very steep and is riprapped with large and jagged rocks. Their adrenaline was evidently still flowing as they hauled their canoes over the rocks and literally threw them down over the other side of the bridge, onto more sharp riprap, and into the water. The thumps and bangs dented the already dented aluminum canoes, and they lay half in and half out of the water. Gil smiled at us and said, "Kind of makes you want to go into the rental business, doesn't it?"

At that point the warden showed up with our wangan, which we sorted out and loaded as the Bostonians searched their stuff for spare cigarettes. In a minute they were sucking contentedly on dry smokes. A cellophane cigarette wrapper blew off the bridge and began its own Allagash voyage.

They then loaded their canoes, which they had pulled completely out of the water on the small, rocky shore below the bridge. Once the loading was done, the stern paddlers got in this was on dry land, mind you and the bow paddlers grabbed the thwarts and dragged the loaded canoes across the beach into the water. The lack of respect they showed for their equipment bespoke their knowledge and is the type of behavior that has cost some people dearly. We finished our lunch as they clunked out of sight, and as there was a headwind blowing and fifty miles of lake paddling ahead, knew we would pass them before they had gone too many miles.

Fifty years ago these folks would not have been able to make this trip. They would have destroyed a wood/canvas canoe, not to mention what they would have done to a birchbark canoe, and I compared their modus operandi to most of the people who have passed through the Allagash it is a good thing that it is a forgiving river.

Fortunately, such groups are not common, especially on Maine's less-well-known rivers, and most people are considerate and careful but even some of them come to grief.

As we study the canoe routes and the way they were used then, we must remember that the people who use them today are vastly different from prehistoric canoeists and those of the pre-paper-company-road era. To understand the canoe routes we have to combine practical experience with thorough research into the documented use by explorers such as Montresor or Chadwick and archaeological data that have been, and will be, produced. It is only in this way that we can come to grips with the topic of ancient canoe use.

I find my greatest enjoyment on the lesser-known canoe rivers and streams of Maine, as they have suffered less the impact of modernity. In the peace and quiet of such old travel ways, it is easy to transport myself back to the old times with an informed imagination.

Often I get the feeling that my poling, paddling, and portaging predecessors are just out of sight around the next bend in the river or ahead of me on a carry trail. In a very real sense this is true. Sigurd Olsen said it best: "When a man is part of his canoe, he is part of all that canoes have ever known."

Notes

Introduction
1. John Jennings (editor), *The Canoe: A Living Tradition*, Toronto: Firefly Books (2002).
2. J. Jennings, "The Realm of the Birchbark Canoe," in *The Canoe* (J. Jennings, ed.) pp. 14–25.
3. Samuel de Champlain, "The Voyages of the Sieurre de Champlain" in *The Works of Samuel de Champlain*, Volume 1, (H. Biggar, ed.), Toronto: The Champlain Society, pp. 338, 39 (1922).
4. Ryan Wheeler, James Miller, Ray McGee, Donna Ruhl, Brenda Swann, and Melissa Memory, "Archaic Period Canoes from Newnans Lake, Florida," *American Antiquity* 68(3): pp. 533–551 (2003).
5. Frank Speck, *Penobscot Man: The Life History of a Forest Tribe in Maine*, Orono: University of Maine Press edition (1997). On page 58 Speck noted, "Gluskabe, the culture hero, is credited [by Native informants] with having introduced the canoe."
6. David Brose, and Issac Greber, "The Ringler Archaic Dugout from Savannah Lake, Ashland County, Ohio, with Speculations on Trade and Transmission in the Prehistory of Eastern United States," *Mid-Continental Journal of Archaeology* 7(2): pp. 245–282 (2002).
7. East coast dugouts were not at all like Pacific northwest coast dugouts which had an entirely different and much more seaworthy design. Westerners added high bows and sterns to increase seaworthiness, adzed the hull for stability, spread the gunwales, and even attached planks on the gunwales to increase freeboard. None of these traits occur in east coast dugouts. See Eugene Arima, "Building Dugouts," in *The Canoe* (J. Jennings, ed.) pp. 96–119 (2002).
8. James Wright, *A History of the Native Peoples of Canada*, Volume I 1 (1,000 BC to AD 50), Mercury Series No. 152, Ottawa: National Museum of Civilization, p 585 (1999);
David Sanger, "Foraging for Swordfish (*Xiphias gladius*) in the Gulf of Maine," in *James V. Wright Memorial Volume*, David Keenlyside (editor), Ottawa: National Museum of Civilization (in press).
9. Sean McGrail, *Boats of the World from the Stone Age to Medieval Times*, New York: Oxford Press (2002).
10. Tappan Adney, and Howard Chapelle, *The Bark Canoes and Skin Boats of North America*, Washington: The Smithsonian Institution (1964).
11. T. Adney, and H. Chapelle, *The Bark Canoes and Skin Boats*.
12. Charles Martijn, *Les Micmac et la Mer*, Montreal: Recherches Amérindiennes au Québec (1986);
Ingeborg Marshall, "Le Canot de Haute Mer des Micmacs" in Martijn (ed.) *Les Micmas et la Mer*, pp. 29–48.
13. For example, close to 9,000 years ago (the Early Archaic period) the drainage of Moosehead Lake changed causing an estimated 15 percent reduction in the Penobscot River flow and a 22percent increase in the Kennebec River. Alice Kelley and David Sanger, "Postglacial Development of the Penobscot River Valley: Implications for Geoarchaeology," in *Geoarchaeology of Landscapes*, (David Cremeens and John Hart, eds.) Albany: New York State Museum, Bulletin 497, pp. 119—133 (2003).
14. Ann Dieffenbacher-Krall, and Andrea Nurse, "Late-Glacial and Holocene Record of Lake Levels of Mathews Pond and Whitehead Lake, Northern Maine, USA," *Journal of Paleolimnology* 34: pp. 283–310 (2005).
15. David Sanger, "An Introduction to the Archaic of the Maritime Peninsula: The

View from Central Maine," in David Sanger, and M. A. P. Renouf (eds) *The Archaic of the Far Northeast*, Orono: University of Maine Press, pp. 221–252 (2006).

16. R. Scott Anderson, George L. Jacobson, Ronald B. Davis, and Robert Stuckenrath "Gould Pond, Maine: Late-Glacial Transitions from Marine to Upland Environments," Boreas, 21:359-371 (1992).

17. Heather Almquist-Jacobson, and David Sanger, "Paleogeographic Changes in Wetland and Upland Environments in the Milford Drainage Basin of Central Maine, in Relation to Holocene Human Settlement History," in *Current Northeast Paleoethnobotany* (John Hart, ed.) Albany: New York State Museum, pp. 177–190 (1999).

18. Arthur Spiess, and John Mosher, "Archaic Hunting and Fishing Around the Gulf of Maine" in *The Archaic of the Far Northeast*, Sanger and Renouf (eds) pp. 383–408 (2006).

19. D. Sanger, "Foraging for Swordfish."

20. Douglas Kellogg, "Why did they Choose to Live Here? Ceramic Period Settlement in the Boothbay, Maine, Region," *Northeast Anthropology* 48: pp. 25–60 (1994);

D. Sanger, "Site Survey and Analysis," in *Landscape Archaeology in the Littoral Zone of Mid-Coast, Maine* (book in preparation).

21. T. Adney, and H. Chapelle, *The Bark and Skin Canoes* (1964).

22. D. Sanger, *Landscape Archaeology* (in prep.).

Preface

1. All the information about Myron Smart has been obtained from Mr. Smart over the last thirty years and is the product of my being the boy next door. My best friend during childhood was Mr. Smart's grandson, Forrest A. Smart, Jr. Many times Myron took us with him into the woods to hunt or fish and sometimes for company while he did his work for the state of Maine. It was on such trips, plus countless hours around his home and canoe shop, that my impressions of the woods and canoes were formed. Other sources of material on the Smart family are noted where used.

2. H. A. Ford, (1882).
3. The Maine Adjutant General's Annual Report for Maine Vol. 2, p. 453.
4. A. G. Hempstead, p. 51 (1931).
5. J. P. Whitten, p. 46 (1976).
6. Ibid., p. 52.
7. Ibid., p. 9.
8. Ibid., p. 6.
9. Ibid., p. 40.
10. F. H. Eckstorm, p. 15 (1941).
11. L. L. Hubbard, p. 206 (1879).
12. Ibid., p. 208.

Chapter One: Land and Water

1. Maine Office of Tourism, Maine.gov site: http://www.state.me.us/ifw/wildlife/watchablewildlife.htm.
2. H. W. Borns, Jr., personal communication.
3. R. B. Davis, T. E. Bradstreet, R. Stuckenrath, H. W. Borns, Jr. (1975).
4. R. Bonnichsen, (1981).
5. M. Lescarbot, (1866).

Chapter Two: The Canoes

1. F. G. Speck, p. 51 (1940).

2. M. G. Levin, and L. P. Potopov, pp. 261, 524, 525, 633, 702, 724, 741, 753 (ND).
3. G. F. MacDonald p. 810 (1982).
4. F. H. Eckstorm, XV.
5. F. Kidder, p. 205 ff (1867).
6. T. Adney, and H. Chappelle, p. 3 (1963).
7. J. Cartier, p. 22 (1914).
8. J. Rosier, p. 105 (1860).
9. Speck, p. 5253.

Chapter Three: Canoeing, Camping, Carrying and Castor Canadensis
1. F. H. Eckstorm, pp. 144, 217, 58.
2. Ibid., p. 15.
3. Ibid., p. 50.
4. Scott Kirby, personal communication.
5. N. Denys, p. 32 (1908).
6. H. D. Thoreau, p. 246 (1961).
7. J. Montresor, pp. 450451.
8. J. A. Maurault, p. 122 (1866).
9. F. H. Eckstorm, p. 20.
10. Ibid., p. 20.
11. Ibid., p. 19.

Chapter Four: The Routes
1. W. G. Wells, p. 73 (1869).
2. Ibid., p. 85.
3. G. A. Wheeler, and H. W. Wheeler (1878).
4. P. Rutherford, p. 92 (1970).
5. W. G. Wells, p. 88 (1869).
6. F. H. Eckstorm, p. 129.
7. Ibid., p. 136, 105.
8. Ibid., p. 144.
9. Ibid., p. 145.
10. Ibid., p. 11.
11. Ibid., p. 13.
12. J. Montresor, p. 15.
13. Ibid., p. 16.
14. C. M. Starbird, p. 52 (1928).
15. J. Montresor, p. 13.
16. R. Bonnichsen, personal communication.
17. F. H. Eckstorm, p. 201.
18. Ibid., p. 201.
19. Ibid., p. 66.
20. Ibid, p. 202.
21. Ibid, p. 65.
22. Ibid., p. 69.
23. W, G. Wells, p. 74 (1869).
24. F. H. Eckstorm, p. 2.
25. Ibid., p. 1.
26. Ibid., p. 1.

27. Ibid., p. 18.
28. Ibid., p. 19.
29. Ibid., p. 20.
30. Ibid., p. 15.
31. Ibid., p. 6.
32. Ibid., p. 22.
33. Ibid., p. 23.
34. Ibid., p. 46.
35. Ibid., p. 31.
36. Joseph Chadwick, p. 1. Much of the following is quoted directly from the text of Chadwick's Survey in *Sprague's Journal of Maine History,* 1928. I have not altered his ingenious spelling and this one note will serve for all the Chadwick material.
37. F. H. Eckstorm, p. 29.
38. Ibid., p. 39.
39. C. L. Borstel, p. 80 (1982).
40. F. H. Eckstorm, p. 41.
41. J. Chadwick, p. 75, Vol. 14, *Sprague's Journal of Maine History,* (1928).
42. F. H. Eckstorm, p. 49.
43. Ibid., p. 49.
44. Michael Brigham, personal communication.
45. J. Chadwick, op. cit.
46. F. H. Eckstorm, p. 162.
47. Donavan D. Drew, personal communication.
48. Greenleaf's Field Book, pp. 16.
49. J. Chadwick, op. cit.
50. F. H. Eckstorm, p. 58.
51. John Gyles, pp. 1 ff.
52. G. F. Clarke, p. 250 (1968).
53. Ibid.
54. L. L. Hubbard, p. 213.
55. Ibid., p. 195.
56. F. H. Eckstorm, p. 63.
57. Ibid.
58. Ibid., p. 204.
59. D. Coffin, and G. Rose, (1829).
60. H. L. Nason, p. 37 (1941).
61. F. H. Eckstorm, p. 62.
62. L. L. Hubbard, p. 197.
63. Ibid., p. 204.
64. A. G. Hempstead, p. 102.
65. F. H. Eckstorm, unpublished material, UMO.
66. L. L. Hubbard, p. 204.
67. Ibid., p. 212.
68. The Maine Rivers Site, http://www.mainerivers.org/st_john.htm.
69. D. Cook, and L. Goldberg, (1983).
70. Arthur Spiess, personal communication.
71. L. L. Hubbard, p. 203.
72. Ibid., p. 196.

Bibliography

The Adjutant General's Annual Report for Maine, 1864, Vol. 2; Augusta, 1865. This series provides an invaluable and in-depth view of the Civil War. Every soldier from Maine is recorded along with his unit and occasional reports of service related activities.

The Appalachian Mountain Club Canoe Guide to New England, third edition. Boston: Appalachian Mountain Club, 1971. This guide has been revised since '71 but is now issued in three separate volumes. This book should be owned by every serious canoeist as it contains much information about canoeability, safety, and accessibility.

Bonnichsen, Robson. "Archaeological Research at Munsungun Lake: Preliminary Technical Report of Activities." Center for the Study of Early Man, Orono, Maine, 1981. This overview represents the multidisciplinary approach to archaeology and details an 11,000-year sequence in interior northern Maine.

Borns, H. W., Jr., P. LaSalle, and W. B. Thompson. "Late Pleistocene History of Northeastern New England and adjacent Quebec." Special Paper 197, Geological Society of America, Boulder, Colorado, 1985. Developed from a symposium in 1981, contains thirteen reports which represent the latest understanding of the end of the last Ice Age.

Borstel, Christopher L. *Archaeological Investigations at the Young Site, Alton, Maine.* Augusta: Maine Historic Preservation Commission, 1982. This site report outlines the archaeological work at the Hirundo/Young site in West Old Town, Maine. Radiocarbon dates and artifacts imply a 5,000-year-old sequence at an inland fishing station.

Bowditch, Henry I. "A Trip to Katahdin." *Appalachia Magazine,* The Appalachian Mountain Club, Dec., 1958; June, 1959, Boston. Bowditch has left an interesting account of a canoe trip down the West Branch Penobscot in the nineteenth century.

Cartier, Jacques. *The Voyages of Jacques Cartier,* Translated by H. P. Bigger, Canadian Archivist Publication #11; 1914. Cartier has left us the first account of birchbark canoes. Those he described must have been the oceangoing version.

Chappelle, Howard I., and Edwin Tappen Adney. *The Bark Canoes and Skin Boats of North America.* The Smithsonian Institution, 1963. This book is a technical manual that is good reading. Data about construction and use of these Native American watercraft is important in understanding function.

Clarke, George F. *Someone Before Us, Our Maritime Indians.* Fredericton, N.B: Brunswick Press, 1968. Clarke was, among other things, an amateur archaeologist. Many of his interpretations are suspected by modern archaeologists but he has left an impressive amount of data regarding St. John River archaeology, especially for those sites now flooded.

Coffin, D., and G. Rose. *Survey Map 1829.* This fragmentary map, in the holdings of the Maine State Library, was drawn after two expeditions (1821 and 1828) to explore the region west of Mars Hill. I have located no field book for the surveys. The map contains Indian place names and portage routes to and from the Aroostook, Allagash, and Penobscot regions in modern Aroostook and Piscataquis counties.

Cook, David, and Lawrence Goldberg. "Munsungun Cherts and Birchbark Canoes." Unpublished paper read at the Society of American Archaeology, Pittsburgh. Center for the Study of Early Man, Orono, 1983. This report discusses the presence of Munsungun chert at various archaeological sites in the Penobscot drainage.

Bibliography

Davis, R. B., T. E. Bradstreet, R. Stuckenrath, H. W. Borns, Jr. "Vegetation and Associated Environments During the Past 14,000 Years Near Moulton Pond, Maine." *Quaternary Research* 5 (1975): 435-465. This important report uses multidisciplinary approach to establish the history of Maine's post-glacial environments.

Denys, Nicholas. *The Description and Natural History of the Coasts of North America.* Translated and edited by W. F. Ganong. Toronto: The Champlain Society, 1908. Denys' account, like those left by other early observers, testifies to the existence of an intricate system of interior canoe routes. He also has left good descriptions of canoes in the Gulf of St. Lawrence.

Eckstorm, Fannie Hardy. *Indian Place Names of the Penobscot Valley and the Maine Coast.* Orono: University of Maine Study Series, Second Series #55, 1941. This book was one of Mrs. Eckstorm's labors of love. While not error free, it remains the single best book on ancient Indian names. Her corrected personal copy of this book is in the Eckstorm material at UMO.

Ford, H. A. *The History of Penobscot County, Maine.* Cleveland, 1882. This dated history records interesting information about the early pioneers on the Penobscot during the Revolutionary Period.

Hempstead, Alfred Geer. *The Penobscot Boom and Improvements on the West Branch for River Driving.* Orono: University of Maine Studies, Second Series #18, 1931. Hempstead has copiously recorded the prodigious dam building done by lumbering and pulp and paper activities on the West Branch and many of its tributaries. The impoundment of water on the waters must have had a deleterious effect on the archaeological remains and should be read by all who are interested in woods history.

Hubbard, Lucius L. *The Woods and Lakes of Maine.* Boston: A. Williams & Company, 1879. Hubbard's book details a lengthy canoe trip where Indian guides, as in Thoreau's and Steele's books, played a vital role. During these trips the guides employed many of the age-old canoe tricks that made travel possible through very difficult terrain. Like Thoreau, Hubbard also recorded many Indian place names.

Kellogg, Edward. Canoeing. Freeport: Published in three volumes by DeLorme Publishing Company, 1958. Zip Kellogg has produced three handy little guides to 50 Maine rivers. Besides technical information he has included fascinating historical data about many sites along their banks.

Kidder, Frederic. *Military Operations in Eastern Maine, and Nova Scotia During the Revolution.* Albany, 1867. Contains the account of Col. Allen and the Maliseet canoe removal to Machias.

Lescarbot, M. *History of New France,* W. L. Grant, Champlain Society, Vol. 11, 1914. One of several seventeenth-century accounts of Indian life of Maine and Maritime Provinces. The Birch canoe is recognized as the primary transportation device. Caution should be used in extending such early ethnographic accounts backward through time.

Levin, M. G., and L. P. Potapov. "The Peoples of Siberia," The University of Chicago Press, Chicago, (no date). This article describes Siberian use of craft much like birchbark canoes. They were poled upstream and portaged, as well as paddled, like the birchbark canoes of the prehistoric Northeast.

MacDonald George F., and Purdy, Barbara A. "Florida's Wet Sites, Where the Past Survives," *Early Man,* (4) 4. Center for American Archaeology, Evanston, IL, (1982): 412. This article provides information regarding the energy-saving aspects associated with the use of dugout canoes in Florida.

Maurault, J. A. *Histoire des Abénakis, Depuis 1605 Jusqu'a Nos Jours.* Gazette de Sorel, 1866. A French history which contains much information from early priests and missionary efforts.

McPhee, John. *The Survival of the Bark Canoe.* New York: Ballantine Books, 1980. John McPhee is one of the most gifted contemporary writers and has documented a modern (1979) canoe trip in "Thoreau country" the headwaters of the West Branch Penobscot. This witty and insightful book should be read by sportsmen and students alike.

Montresor, John. *Montresor's Journal.* Reprinted in the Collections of the Maine Historical Society, Volume One. Montresor was an intrepid scout and soldier of the Crown. His Journal is the best account of the Kennebec/Quebec canoe route and associated hardships.

Nason, Harold L. "Canoeing the Little East Branch of the Penobscot," *In the Maine Woods.* The Bangor and Aroostook Railroad, Bangor, 1941. Nason has written an interesting and well illustrated article about his travel over an old Allagash/East Branch Penobscot canoe route. Little used in modern times, Nason describes a rugged trip.

Rosier, James. *Rosier's Narrative of Waymouth's Voyage to the Coast of Maine in 1605, with Remarks by George Prince: Showing the River Explored to Have Been the George's River.* Bath: 1860. Contains interesting observations of Maine Indians and their canoes.

Rutherford, Phillip. *A Dictionary of Maine Place Names.* Cumberland Press, 1970.

Snow, Dean R. *A Summary of Excavations at the Hathaway site in Passadumkeag, Maine, 1912, 1947, & 1968.* Orono: Department of Anthropology, University of Maine. This is an example of an archaeological study of one important riverine site on the Penobscot. This site shows human occupation of this site for at least six thousand years.

Speck, Frank G. *Penobscot Man.* University of Pennsylvania Press; 1940. This book was the standard for North American anthropology for many years. Speck was a close observer of the Woodland tribes and has left several other important studies of this nature.

Starbird, Charles M. *Indians of the Androscoggin Valley.* Lewiston, 1928. This book provides some interesting, though not always reliable, information on tribes of the Androscoggin, including place names and anecdotes.

Steele, Thomas Sedgewick. *Canoe and Camera and Pole, Paddle and Portage.* Boston: Estes & Lauriat, 1882. Birchbark canoe travel in the nineteenth century with many excellent illustrations of the country, the canoes, and the "wangan."

Thomas, Eben. The Weekender. Hallowell: 1979. One of a series of handy canoe guides by a modern canoe enthusiast. Technical information is provided along with logistical suggestions and many excellent photos and maps.

Thoreau, Henry D. *The Maine Woods.* New York: Thomas Y. Crowell & Company, 1961. Thoreau has the reputation as being the first "out of stater." He has left us a lyrical account of his three sojourns in Maine during the 1840s and 1850s.

Wheeler, George A., and Henry W. Wheeler. *History of Brunswick, Topsham and Harpswell, Main, Including the Ancient Territory Known as Pejepscot.* Brunswisk, 1878.

Wells, Walter G. *The Water Power of Maine.* Augusta: 1869. This hydrographic survey of Maine waterways is a valuable guide to the rivers of Maine.

Whitten, Jeanne Patten. *Fannie Hardy Eckstorm: A Descriptive Bibliography.* Orono: The Northeast Folklore Society, The University of Maine, 1976. This is a valuable guide to the Eckstorm papers which are in Fogler Library at the University of Maine.

Bibliography

Willoughby, Charles C. *Indian Antiquities of the Kennebec Valley: An Occasional Publication in Maine Archaeology #1*. The Maine Historic Preservation Commission and the Maine State Museum. This book is a reproduction of a beautiful book designed and given by Willoughby to his daughter. Willoughby was an artist and antiquarian who became a professional anthropologist in his mid-thirties. This book has an informative text but its strength is the color plates that Willoughby did of artifacts found along the length of the Kennebec. These paintings are so well done that archaeologists today can identify the lithic material they were made from and the flaking method used to produce them.

Winship, George P. Sailors Narratives of Voyages Along the New England Coast, 1525-1624. Boston: Houghton-Mifflin & Company, 1905. This is a helpful collection of early accounts of Europeans of importance to this study.

Index

Abagadassett River 59
Abagadusset Point 38
Abbott Academy 11
Abenaki 43
Abol Stream 94
Aboljackarmegas rapids 95
Adirondacks 53
Adney, Edwin Tappan 21
agate 52
agwiden, "floats lightly" 23
ahwangan 9
Alamoosook Lake 72
alder 49
Alexies, Sac (Jacques Alexis) 75
Allagash (village) 109
Allagash Falls 109
Allagash Lake 110, 111
Allagash Lakes 105
Allagash lakes 91-93, 104-5, 111
Allagash Pond 110
Allagash River 1, 99, 105, 108-10, 112-13, 118-19, 121
    first section 109
    Mud Pond Carry 115
Allagash Waterway 119
Allagash Wilderness Waterway 109, 111
Allan, Colonel John 23, 101
Amascontee, "plenty of alewives" 64
Ambajejus Lake 83
Ambajejus rapids 95
Ambejackmockamus rapids 95
American Civil War 5
American Ornithologists' Union 11
anadromous fish 67
Andover, Massachusetts 11
Androscoggin headwaters 64
Androscoggin Lake 58
Androscoggin, "place for curing fish" 12
Androscoggin River 18, 32, 51, 56, 58-59
    Little Androscoggin River 57
Androscoggin watershed 56
Annabessacook Lake 58
Appalachian chain 99
Appalachian Trail 94
Appleton 67
Archaic period xvii
Arnold expedition 46, 64
Aroostook River 3, 90-92, 99, 104-8
Aroostook, "the beautiful river" 91, 104

Aroostook watershed 109
arrowheads 83
ash 16
Ashland 3, 109
Aspequent, Joseph 75, 78
Attean, Joseph xi
Attean Pond 64
Aukpaque 101
Avery Brook 48
Aziscohos Lake 58

Bagaduce River 69
Bagaduce Road 48
Baker Lake 48, 98, 110
Bangor 5, 7, 60, 71-72
Bangor School of Commerce 10
Banks, John ix
Bar Harbor Road 49
Baskahegan Stream 88, 90
Baskahegan Stream, "a branch stream" 90
Bay of Chaleur 92, 99, 106
Bay Path 19
Bear River 58
beaver 47-50, 52, 62, 73, 77-78, 92, 98, 111
    Quorbeduk beaver dam 47
Beaver Brook 105
Beaver Cove 85
Becancour River 31
beech 16
Belfast 60, 68
Belfast Bay 69
Belgrade Lakes 59
Benjamin River 69
Benson Pond 84
Betula papyrifera 2
Big Ambejackmockamus Falls 96, 111
Big Black River 112-13
Big Bog 98
Big Eddy 96
Big Lake 90, 101
Bingham 21
birch xv-xviii, 2, 16, 26, 65
birch bark xv-xviii, 2, 18, 21, 27-28, 79, 89, 110
birchbark canoe xv-xx, 30, 84
Birch Island x
Birch Stream x, xii
black spruce 21

Index

Blackman Stream 49, 73
Blake Hill 48
Blue Hill 68
Blue Hill Falls 69
Bodfish Intervale 85
Bodfish, Samuel 85
Bonnichsen, Robson 3, 67
Boothbay xx
Boston 23
Bradley 49
Branch Lake 72
Brassua 5
Brassua Lake 8
Brewer 11, 49, 72
Brewer Lake 72
Broad Sound 68
Brooklin 69
Brownville 38
Brunswick 56-57
Buck's Cove 84
Bucksport 68, 72
bullboats 22, 29, 89

Camden 68
Camden Harbor 69
Campbell Lake 81
Canada Falls 99
Canada Falls Deadwater 99
canoe
   aluminum 119
   bark canoe 22, 26-27
   birchbark canoe 1-2, 12, 18, 21-23, 26
   dugout canoe xvi-xvii, xix, 18, 22-23
   moosehide canoe xvii, 29
   ocean canoe 26, 29
   of elm and oak bark 29
   Old Town Tripper 119
   pack canoe 27
   river canoe 27
   seventeen-foot Old Town 119
   Smart River Queen 119
   temporary canoes 29
   woods canoe 27
cant dog 7
Cape Cod 18
Cape Rosier xii-xiii, 69
Caratunk 63
Caratunk Falls archaeological site 114
Caratunk Falls Dam 114
Caribou Lake 96-97
Carrabassett River 64
carries 32, 40-42, 49

above The Forks 60
across peninsulas 68
Allagash Falls 109
Androscoggin to Cathance Pond 57
Androscoggin to Cobbosseecontee
   system 57-58
Baskahegan portages 90
Beaver Brook to Fish River 105
Benson Pond to Onawa Lake 84
Big Bog to Fifth St. John Pond 98
Big Lake to East Machias River 101
Castine Neck 69
Caucomgomoc Lake to Baker Lake 48
Chase's Rips 111
Chaudière to Penobscot Brook 44
Coombs Cove to West Branch of Carry
   Brook 91
East Branch carries 43
Ellis River to Rangeley Lakes 58
from Gassabias to Fourth Machias
   Lake 81
from head of Campbell Lake 81
from lower Androscoggin 57
Horserace 111
into north-flowing Carry Brook 86
into the Punchbowl 69
into Thurston Pond 72
into Wilson Pond 58
Little Bog to Sweeney Brook 98
Little Machias River to Fish River 105
Mattawamkeag to Meduxnekeag 90
Mattawamkeag to St. Croix Stream 90
Mattawamkeag's West Branch to East
   Branch Penobsc 90
Metagamoughschesh 88
Metagmoughschesh 102
Millinocket Portage 92
Millinocket Stream to East Branch
   Penobscot and Allagash lakes 105
Mud Brook 95
Mud Pond 92
Mud Pond Carry 108, 115
Muddy/Androscoggin/Cathance 57
Negas 72
Newnan's Lake xvi
Northeast Carry 33, 93, 97
Northeast or Northwest 83
Northwest Carry 13, 47, 86, 93, 97
Old Town's Main Street 78
Ooniganissek 69
original Chesuncook/Ripogenus 96
Osgood Carry 108

Index

Passadumkeag 80
Penobscot Pond 94
Penobscot River to Moosehead 97
Penobscot to Chiputneticook Lake 88
Pollywog Pond 93
Portage Lake 107
Portage Lake to Penobscot Lake 44
Presque Isle Stream to Prestile/Meduxnekeag 104
Ship Pond Stream 84
Spencer Stream to Moose River 64
St. John brooks 110
St. John to Long Lake 107
Stevens Carry 57
"the Carry", Eagle Lake to Square Lake 107
to and from Long Pond 85
to Cuxabexis Stream 95
to Four Sabaos 81
to Harrington Lake 95
to Indian Pond 85
to South Branch of Marsh River 72
to St. Croix Stream 104
to Sysladobsis Lake 81
Twin Brook Falls 109
upper Allagash Stream 110
Upper Carrying Place 56
Wadleigh Deadwater 91
West Branch falls 95
West Branch Machias via Campbell Lake 81
West Branch to Ripogenus Lake 95
Carry Brook 62-63
Carry Brook, West Branch 91
Carry Pond 104, 107
Carry Ponds 64
Carrying Place Cove 59
Cartier, Jacques 26-27
Casco Bay 57
Castine 32
Castine Neck 68
Cathance River 59
Caucomgomoc 9
Caucomgomoc Lake 1, 111
  "Big Gull Lake" 48
Caucomgomoc Stream 97
cedar 22, 28
cedar rails 27
cedar ribs 27
cedar "shoes" 108
Center for the Study of the First Americans (CSFA) 105

Chadwick, Joseph 47, 50, 73, 75-76, 78-79 80-81, 83-87, 93-94, 96
Chadwick survey, 1764 73, 76
Chaleur, Bay of 26
Chamberlain Lake 92, 108, 110-11, 115-16
  Apmoo'gene gamook, "the lake that is crossed" 115
Charlie's Corner 5
Chase Brook 108
Chase Lake 108
Chase's Rapids 119
Chase's Rips 110-11
Chaudière headwaters 64, 97
Chaudière River 18, 32, 43
Chaudière watershed 58
Chaudière/Penobscot/Kennebec route 13
Chemo Lake 73
Chemquasabamticook "stream that runs from the mountains" 110
Chemquasabamticook Lake 110
Chemquasabamticook Stream 110
Cherokee x
chert 65, 106
  Christmas tree 106
  East Branch Penobscot 106
  Grand Lake Matagamon 106
  Munsungan 3, 67, 105-6, 109
  Norway Bluff and Round Mountain 17
  Round Mountain 105
Chesuncook Lake 86, 95-97, 116
Chesuncook Village 116
Chicago 11
Chimenticook Stream 112
Chimskiticook, "big deadwater" 13
China Lake 59
Chiputneticook Lakes 90, 101
Churchill Dam 118
Churchill Lake 110-11, 118
Churchill Lake dam 110
Ciss Stream 111
Clark, George Frederick 88
Clovis fluted points 106
Cobbossee 59
  "where they spear sturgeon by torchlight" 12
Cobbossee Stream 59
Cobbosseecontee, "where they spear sturgeon by torchlight" 37
Cobbosseecontee system 58
Cochnewagon Lake, "the closed-up route" 58
Coffin, George W. 92-93

Index

Coffin, Paul 32
Colby, Howard 117-18
Cold River 56
Connecticut River 6, 18-19, 32, 56, 58
Connecticut River Log Drive 5
Coopers Mills 67
Corps de Afrique 5
Cowan, Frank 117
Crawford, William 75
Cross Lake 107
Crowne's Point 72
Cupsuptic River 58
Cushnoc, "the head of tide" 60
cutoffs xx, 59
Cuxabexis Stream 95

Daaquam River 112
Daicey Pond 95
Damariscotta River 67-68
Davenport Cove 88
de Champlain, Samuel xvi, 30, 38
Dead Diamond River 58
Dead River 32, 58, 60, 64, 72
Dead River, South Branch 58
Dead River system 62
Dead Stream 58
deadwater 13
Debsconeag Ponds 93
Debsconeag rapids 95
Deerfield Valley 19
Delesdernier, Lt. Lewis Frederick 101
Denys, Nicholas 28, 39
Dickey-Lincoln Hydroelectric Dam Project 113
Doshen shore 68-69
Down Street x
Drake Brook 110
Draper Pond 95
Druillettes, Gabriel 45-47

Eagle Lake 81, 92, 117
East and West Shirley bogs 86
East Grand Lake 90
East River 68
Eastern Avenue 48
Eastern River 59, 67
Eastford, CT 19
Eaton Brook 48, 72
Eber's Point x
Echo Lake 108
Eckstorm, Fannie Hardy xi, 10-12, 14
Eckstorm, Jacob A. 11

Edali-chichiquasik, "where it is very narrow" 69
Edali-si-back emuck "where they waited for the tide" 69
Edaweit, Messer 75
Eddington Bend 48, 72
Eel Lake 88
Eel River 101
Eggemoggin Reach, "the fish weir place" 69
Ellis Brook 111
Ellis Pond 111
Ellis River 58
Ellsworth 72
Eskers 17
eskers 17
Evenks 21
Everglades 22

Farmington Falls 64
felsite 65, 105
    Kineo felsite 52-53, 67
Felt Brook 49, 72
Fifth St. John Pond 98
Finlay, Hugh 44-45, 98
fir 16
First Musquash Pond 94
Fish River 99, 104-8
Fish River Lake 107
Fisher Brook 48
Fisher Mill Stream 48
Fisher Stream 48
flint 65
Fogler Library 10
Fort Dawson x
Fort Kent 106
Fort Point 69
Fort Pownall 73, 75
Four Sabaos 81
Fourth Machias Lake 81
Fowler Carry 42
Francis 76
French and Indian Wars 80
French Recollets 112
Fryeburg 32
Fundy, Bay of 32, 52
    archaeological expedition 53

Game Division of the Department of Inland Fisherie 10
Ganong, Dr. William Francis 11, 104, 112
Gassabias Lake 81

Index

Gassabias Lake, "Little clear-water lake" 81
getting sluiced 8
gikque' mkwahque, "prods under the water" 28
Gilpatrick, Gil 120
glacier 16
Gluskabe xii
Goldthwait, Thomas 75
Goodblood, Joe 116
Goose Falls 69
Gouges xvii
Graham Lake 73
Grand Falls 42, 81, 89, 101
Grand Lake 103
Grand Lake Matagamon 91, 106
Grand Lake Road 91
Grand Lake Seboeis 91
Grand Manan 54-55
Great Depression 12
Great Falls, Machias River 37
Great Falls, Old Town 71
Great Northern Paper Company 6
Great Works Stream 73
Green Lake 72
Green Point Road 49
Greenleaf, Ebenezer 85
Greenleaf, Moses 85
Gulf of Maine 30, 52
Gulf of St. Lawrence 106
Gyles, John 87-89, 90

Hardy, Jeremiah P. 10
Hardy, Manly 10, 48
Harrington Lake 95
Hartshorne, Elizabeth 65
Hatch Cove 69
Hay Brook 92
Haymock Lake 92
headboard 28
hemlock 16
Hemlock Island x, xii
Hemlock Stream xii
Hen and Chickens 5
Henderson boys 9
Herring Cove 53
Hirundo and the Young Sites 80
Holbrook Pond 49
Holbrooks Island 69
Holden Meeting House 48
Holyoke 6
horsebacks 17
Horserace 111

Horseshoe Cove 69
Houlton 88
Howland 83
Hubbard, Lucius L. 93, 115, 117
    The Woods and Lakes of Maine 108
Hungry Meadow 48
"hunk" 13

Indian Island ix-x, 78-79
Indian Pitch 42
Indian Pond 62-63
Indian Trails of Maine 11
Indian Wars 18-19, 87
Iroquois 29
Islesboro Island xiii
isostatic rebound 17, 21

Jefferson, town of 67
Jesuits 51, 112
Jo-Mary lakes 83
Joe Merry Lake 9
Joe Pease Rapids ix
Johnson, Arthur 5
Jolliet, Louis 30

Kaghskibinday, "cedars" 72
kames 17
Katahdin, Mount 86, 94-95, 99
Katahdinough 99
kayak 21
Kebec, "where the river narrows" 59
Kellogg Lumber Company 7
Kenduskeag, "eel weir place" 38
Kenduskeag Stream 38, 60, 72
Kenduskeag, "the eel weir place" 72
Kennebec Indians 86
Kennebec, "long water place" 59
Kennebec River 18, 21, 32, 51, 56, 59, 62-3, 80, 86, 94, 114
Kennebec River, East Outlet on Moosehead Lake 60
Kennebec, "the long reach" 12
Kennebec valley 17
Kennebec watershed 38, 58
Kezar River 56
Khants 21
Kiasobeak 81
Kiasobeak, "clear water lake" 81
Kidney Pond 95
Kineo House 117
Kineo, Mount 64
Knox Island 3

Index

Krepner, Mike 53-54

La Hontan, Louis-Armand de Lom
   d'Arce, baron de 29
La Pomkeag Stream 105
La Pomkeag Stream, "rope stream" 91
Lachine Rapids 30
Lawrence Bay 69
Lescarbot, Marc 18
Linière River 43
Little Black River 112
Little Bog 98
Little Falls, Machias River 37
Little Madawaska River 104
Little Shallow Pond 111
Little Spencer Stream 58
log kettle 38
Lola, Henry 6
Long Lake 107
Long Pond 84-85
longboat 26
Loron, Penobscot Chief 23
Lower Lakes 93-94
Lower Lakes, West Branch Penobscot 83

Machias, "bad little rapids" 37
Machias River 37, 42, 81, 90, 101, 105
   Little Machias River 105
Machias River, East Branch 81
Machias River, West Branch 81
Madamiscontis, "plenty of alewives" 12
Madawamkee (Mattawamkeag) 87
Madawaska Lake 107
Madawescook (Madawaska) 89
Madunkehunk, "height of land stream" 13
Maine State Library 12
Maine Volunteer Infantry, 13th Regiment 5
Maliseets ix, 29, 70, 87, 89, 101
Mansi 21
Mantawassuc, "inlet" 48
Mantawassuc Stream 48
maple 16
maple sugar 79
maple trees 71
Maquoit Bay 56
Marey, Joseph 76
Marquette, Jacques 30
Mars Hill 92
Marsh Island 73, 79
Marsh River 72
Mary Ann 6
Masardis 90

Massachusetts 6
Massachusetts Bay 19
Matagamon (Second Lake) 92
Matagamon Lake 42, 91-93
Mat'chi-wis'is, "the bad falls" 78
Mattawamkeag 83
Mattawamkeag, "at the mouth a gravel
   bar" 37
Mattawamkeag, East Branch 90
Mattawamkeag River 80, 87, 90, 105
Mattawamkeag system 104
Mattawamkeag village 88
Mattawamkeag, West Branch 90
Maurault, J. A. 46
Medomac River 67
Meductic 88, 101
Meductic, "at the end of the trail" 88
Meductic Intervale 88
Meduxnekeag River 89, 99, 103, 104-5
   "where the people come out" 90
Meduxnekeag River, South Branch 104
Megantic, Lake 58
Megkwakagarnik, "Mud Pond" 115
Megunticook Lake 69
Merrimac 56
Merrymeeting Bay 38, 56, 59
Messalonskee Stream 60
Micmacs ix, 29-39, 70
midden xix, xx
Millinocket 21, 42
Millinocket Lake 83, 92
Millinocket Stream 42, 105
Milo 83
minke whale 54
Minnewokon, "the many directions
   route" 69
Mohawk Island 80
Mohawk Trail 19
Mohawks 43, 45, 80
Monhegan Island 53
Montresor, Colonel John 43, 46-47, 60,
   62-65, 73, 76, 98
Moorehead Phase 52
moose hide 29, 46, 89
Moose Pond 92
Moose River 5, 7-8, 58, 63, 64
Moose River drive 10
Moosehead artifacts 65
Moosehead Lake 5, 7-8, 13, 23, 40, 58-59,
   60, 62-65, 83, 85-86, 94, 97, 108
Moosehead Lake archaeology 65, 67
Moosehead Lake, East Outlet 63

Index

Moosehorn Stream 72
Mooseleuk Stream 105
Mount Desert Island 72
Mount Kineo 105
Mousam River 56
Mud Brook 95
Mud Pond 92, 95, 115
Mud Pond Carry 115-18
Munsungan
   chert 3, 67, 105, 106, 109
   CSFA study 105
   Munsungan Lake 1, 105, 108
   Munsungan Project 106
   Munsungan Stream 105
   Paleo-Indian site 3
Murphy, Cornelius "Con" 5
Murray, James 76, 78
Muscongus Bay 59
Muskrat Brook 72
Musquacook, "birch-bark place" 110
Musquacook Deadwater 109
Musquacook lakes 105, 108
Musquacook Stream 105, 109
Musquash (Muskrat) River 90
Myron Smart 98

Nahmadunkehunk, the "height of land stream" 93, 96
Nahmakanta Lake, "where there are plenty of lake trout" 93
Nanays 21
Narraguagus River 42, 81
Narramissic River 49
Nason, Harold 92
National Ocean and Atmospheric Administration 55
Nautilus Island 69
Neganodenek 78
Negas 72-73
Nemutchinoetegus Stream 92
Neptune, Assong (Chief John Neptune) xi, 75
Nesowadnehunk, "stream that runs between the mountains" 13
Nesowadnehunk Deadwater 95
Nesowadnehunk Falls 96
Nesowadnehunk rapids 95
Nesowadnehunk Stream 95, 96
New Brunswick 12, 17, 53, 83, 99, 106, 108
New Brunswick Museum 14
New Hampshire 6, 83

New Harbor 68, 87
New Meadows River 56, 59
Nicatou, "where the route splits" 90
Nicatou Island xi
Nicatous 81
Nicatous Lake 81
Nicatous Stream 81
Nicatowis 90
Nicatowis, "little fork" 81
Nicholas, Louie 98
Nicholas, Roy 9
Nineteenth Century Club of Bangor 11
Nipmuck Path 19
Norridgewock 5, 32, 64
North Adams, MA 19
North and South Twin Lakes 83
North Branch Penobscot 76
North Branch Penobscot Chaudiere route 23
North Haven 53
North Lake 88
Northeast Carry 40, 117
Northern Forest Canoe Trail 53
Northwest Carry 65
Northwest Passage 30
Norway Bluff 3, 17, 106
Norwich, CT 19
Notre Dame Mountains 89
Nova Scotia 18, 52-55
Nuton, Philop (Phillip Newton) 75

oak 16
Oak Hill x
Obernecksombeek Pond 84
Olamon Island, "red clay (or paint)" xii
Olamon Stream 73, 80
Old Town x, 7, 11, 23, 60, 71, 73, 78, 80, 83
Olsen, Sigurd 122
Onawa Lake 84
Oodoolseezicook-Ahwangan "the Entrails Pond route" 13
Oodoolseezicook-Ahwangan, "the Entrails Pond route" 96
Oodoolwagenow-seezicook Ahwangan "the Entrails Route" 96
Ooniganissek, "the short carry" 69
Orcutt Harbor 69
Oregon 19
Orland River 72
Orochi 21
Orono xi, 73

Index

Orson Bog 73
Orson Island x, 73
Ossipee River 56
 Little Ossipee River 56
O'zwazo-ge-hunk "when they come by here they wade their canoes" 13

Paleo-era 38
Paleo-Indians xix, 16, 17, 21, 22
Passadumkeag, "above the gravel bar" xii
Passadumkeag forks 81
Passadumkeag River 80-81, 83
Passadumkeag Stream 73
Passagassawakeag region 60
Passagassawaukeag (Passagassawassakeag) River, "where they speared sturgeon by torchlight" xii, 69
Passamagamet rapids 95
Passamaquoddy ix, 70
Passamaquoddy Bay 81, 87
Passamaquoddy Indians 29
Peavey 10
Peavey, Joseph 7
Pejepscot Falls 56
Pejepscot, "long rocky rapids part" 56
Pemadumcook Lake 83, 93
Pemaquid 87
Pemaquid Point 68
Pemtegwa'took, "main river" 70
Penobscot "the rocky place," "the descending ledge place" 70
Penobscot Bay 3, 53, 59, 68-70, 72, 106
Penobscot Brook 14, 44
Penobscot country 13
Penobscot Lake 13, 44, 98
Penobscot Pond 94
Penobscot ponds 111
Penobscot region 10, 23
Penobscot River ix-xiii, 5, 13, 18, 21, 29, 38, 42, 48-49, 51, 70, 72-73, 80-81, 83, 86-87, 98, 105, 116
 Bangor Salmon Pool 71, 78
 East Branch 11, 34, 42, 90, 91, 93, 105, 106, 116
 little East Branch (above Matagamon) 42, 92
 little East Branch Penobscot (above Matagamon) 93
 Mud Pond Carry 115
 North Branch 98
 Pannawambskek, "where the ledges spread out" 71
 Pemtegwa'took, "main river" 70
 South Branch 98
 West Branch 1, 5, 9, 11, 13, 40, 42, 76, 91-97, 105, 108, 111, 117
 Kettetegwewick, "the main Branch" 93
Penobscot River system 70
Penobscot routes 70
Penobscot Salmon Pool 5
Penobscot system 99
Penobscot, the forks 90
Penobscot valley 17
Penobscot watershed 13, 45, 106
Penobscot Woods 7
Penobscots ix-xiii, 6, 9, 11, 23, 28, 70, 73, 75-76, 78, 80, 98
Pequot Path 19
Pesutamesset, "seen only when near it" 49, 72
Phillips Lake 49, 72
Phillips Mill Stream 48
Pinchgut Branch 48
Pinchgut Brook 48
Pinus rigida 18
Piscataqua River 18
Piscataquis 9
Piscataquis Ahwangan 3, 9, 32, 38, 60, 76, 83, 86
Piscataquis Ahwangan, archaeological sites 86
Piscataquis County 73
Piscataquis, "little branch stream" 83
Piscataquis region 64
Piscataquis River 38, 60, 80, 83-84, 86, 93
Piscataquis System 86
Piscataquis, the forks 83
Pistol Green 81
pitch pine 18
pitching the seams 28
Pittston Farm 97-98
Plano-style 38
Pleasant Lake 108
Pleasant River 9, 38, 83-84, 93
Polis, Joe xi, 40
Pollywog Pond 93
Pollywog Stream 94
poplar 16
Port Royal Annapolis 18
Portage Lake 44, 105, 107
portages 41
Preble, John 73, 75
Presque Isle Stream 104

Index

Prestile River 104
Prestile Stream 104
Presumpscot River 56
Presumpscot system 56
Priestly Lake, Awanganis, "the little route" 110
Prince Edward Island 26
prisoners of war 65
Providence, RI 19
Punchbowl 69
Puritans 46
Pushaw Stream 60, 79

Quakish Lake 42
quartering 54
quartz 84
Quebec 6, 17-18, 23, 30, 32, 76, 112

Rafts 29
Railroad Chesuncook, Chamberlain and Eagle Lake 117
Ranco, Ed 117
Rangeley Lakes 56, 58
rawhide 46
red pine 16
Red River 107, 108
Revolutionary War 64, 101
Rhode Island 11
Rip Dam 96
Ripogenus Dam 96
Ripogenus Gorge 96
Ripogenus Lake 95, 96-97
Ripogenus Stream 95
Roach River 94
Rockwood, Maine 6
Rommel's Afrika Korps 65
Rose, Daniel 92, 93
Rosier, James 26
Ross, John 5
Round Mountain 106
    chert 3, 17, 105
Round Pond 68, 109
routes 49, 56
    Allagash and upper St. John 109
    Allagash lakes 111
    Aroostook River from St. John 104
    Aroostook tributary 107
    ascending the Piscataquis to Moosehead 86
    "back door" of the Fish River 107
    Baskahegan to Meduxnekeag 88
    between Maine and Quebec 76
    between Sebasticook and Penobscot 76
    Blackman Stream to Union River country 73
    Buck's Cove 84
    Bucksport to Blue Hill region 68, 69
    Camden to Belfast 68
    Carrabassett 64
    Carry Brook 62
    Castine Neck to Eggemoggin Reach 69
    categories 51
    Chemquasabamticook Stream (Sebemsicook Stream) 110
    Chiputneticook/Eel River 88, 101
    cutoffs 51, 70
    Damariscotta River to New Harbor 68
        to Broad Sound 68
        to Round Pond 68
    Dead River 58, 64
    Dead River/Spencer Stream 63
    down the West Branch to Chesuncook 86
    Drake Brook 110
    Druillettes' route 45
    Ellis Brook 111
    Felt and Eaton brooks 72
    Finlay's route 45
    from Aziscohos Lake 58
    from Brewer Lake 72
    from middle Androscoggin River 58
    from Rangeley Lakes to Kennebec watershed 58
    from Rangeley Lakes to Moose River 58
    Kenduskeag Stream 72
    Kennebec to Moosehead Lake 60
    Kennebec to Piscataquis Ahwangan 86
    Kennebec/ Penobscot Bay 68
    Kennebec/Dead River/Chaudiere 64
    Kennebec/Dead River/Chaudière 46
    Kennebec/Rangeley Lakes/Androscoggin 64
    Kokadjo-weengwa-sebemsis-ahwangan 93
    lower Penobscot 71
    Machias River system/Scraggly Lake 90
    main Kennebec 63
    major routes 51
    Malecites with Col. Allen 101
    Matagamon Lake to Aroostook River 92

Matagamon Lake to Bay of Chaleur 92
Mattawamkeag 90
Mattawamkeag canoe route 87
Mattawamkeag to St John 88
Meduxnekeag 89, 103
   Aroostook 104
   Mattawamkeag system 104
   St. Croix River 104
Messalonskee Stream to Belgrade Lakes 60
middle Kennebec bypass 59
Montresor's route 45
Mud Pond/Allagash approach 92
Musquacook Stream 109
Musquash (Muskrat) River to Big Lake 90
neighborhood routes 52, 56
Nicatous Stream to Passamaquoddy Bay 81
nine Aroostook options 104
North Branch Penobscot 98
northeastern canoe route network 70
Oodoolseezicook-Ahwangan, "the Entrails Pond route" 13
Oodoolwagenow-seezicook Ahwangan, "Entrails Route" 95
Ooniganissek 69
Orland River/Union River watershed 72
Outlet Stream to China Lake 60
Passadumkeag River 80
Passagassawaukeag River to Camden Harbor 69
Passagassawaukeag/St. Georges/ east 69
Penobscot Bay to Lubec 68
Penobscot, East and West Branches 90
Penobscot/Union River 73
Piscataquis Ahwangan 83, 86
Piscataquis and Sebec River approach to Moosehead 83
Prestile Stream 104
Pushaw Stream 80
Red River 107
Sandy River to Belgrade/Kennebec lake system 64
Sebasticook "the short route" 13
Sebasticook River 60
Sebasticook/Penobscot 67
Sebec River 84
Sebec River approach 86
Sebec up to Onawa Lake 85

Sheepscot River to coastal bays 59
short routes 51, 56
Souadabscook Stream 72
South Branch Penobscot 98
St. John tributaries 99
St. John tributaries to St. Lawrence valley 112
St. Lawrence to the Gulf of Maine 99
subroutes within the Fish River system 107
Sweeny Brook 98
Swift and Bear rivers 58
Telos Cut 93
The Kokadjo-weengwa-sebemsis-ahwangan 94
to and from Penobscot Bay 70
Tobique River to Bay of Chaleur 106
Tomah Stream to East Grand Lake 90
up Dead River/Moosehorn Stream 72
up Lawrence Bay 69
up Muskrat Brook 72
upper Kennebec 63
upper St. John to Penobscot 98
Wadleigh Deadwater 91
Webster Stream 93
Wesserunsett Stream 64
West Branch approach to Moosehead 83
West Branch of Carry Brook 91
West Branch/Moosehead Lake/Kennebec connections 93
West Outlet Stream 63
Royal River 56

Sabattus Stream 58
Sabtes (Jean Baptiste) 76
Saco, "a stream of water" 12
Saco River 18, 51, 56
Saco watershed 56
Sagadahoc, "where the river runs in" 59
Saint Croix Stream 105
Salmon Falls 56
Sand Bar Point, Moosehead Lake 65
Sandy Bay Township 7
Sandy Beach ix
Sandy Point 72
Sandy River 64
Sanger, David 3, 52-53, 56
Satinhungemoss Hill (Katahdin) 94
Savannah Lake xvi
Schoodic Lake 73
Schoodic Lakes 90

Index

Schoodic Stream 38
Schoodic, "trout place" 38
Scraggly Lake 90
Sears Island (aka Brigadier's Island) 69
Sebago Lake 57
Sebago Lake, "the big lake" 56
Sebamook, "a large body of water" 93
Sebasticook River 38, 60, 72, 80, 86
Sebasticook, "the short route" 13, 60
Sebec 5
Sebec, "a large body of water" 84
Sebec archaeological sites 84
Sebec Lake 84
Sebec River 83-84, 86
Sebem, Lake (Moosehead) 85
Sebemsicook Lake 110
Sebemsicook Stream (Chemquasabamticook Stream) 110
Seboeis Lake 105
Seboeis River 91, 105
Seboeis Stream 83-84, 93
Seboomook 47, 97
Seboomook Lake 97
Second Connecticut Lake 6
Second Musquash Pond 94
Second Roach Pond 94
Sededunkehunk, "rapids at the mouth" 13
Sedgeunkedunk Stream 72
Sedgwick 69
setting poles 33
Sheepscot Bay 59
Sheepscot River 59, 67
Shin Pond 91
Ship Pond Stream 84
Siberia 21
skin boat 22
Skiticook, "a deadwater" 13
Skowhegan 63
Slaughter Pond 95
Smart, Bill 5-6
Smart canoe 91
Smart, Captain James L. 5
Smart, Frank 5-7, 9
Smart, John 5
Smart, Myron 4, 7-8, 10, 35
Smith, Ansel 116
Smith, Bill 92
Smith Brook 92
Smith, Captain John 26
Smith College 11-12
Smith, Frank 117
Smith, Jr., Ansel 116

Smyrna Mills 104
Snake Bog 92-93
snub man 8
snubber 8
snubbing downriver 63
Sock's Island 80
Soper Brook 95
Souadabscook Stream 60, 67
Souadabscook Stream, "at the sloping ledge" 72
Spencer Stream 64
Spider Lake 108
Spiess, Arthur 3
sprinkler 7
spruce 16
spruce bark 79
spruce gum 28
spruce root 27-28
St. Croix River 42, 81, 87-88, 101, 104
    West Branch 101
St. Croix Stream 90, 104
St. Croix watershed, lower Lakes 90
St. Francis River 30, 112
St. Froid Lake 107
St. George River 67-68
St. Georges River 69
St. John brooks 110
St. John ponds 98, 112
St. John River 9, 18, 51, 88-89, 98-99, 101, 104-7
    Baker Branch 98
    headwaters 89, 97
    lower 22, 83, 87, 90, 101
    Southwest Branch 46, 112
    upper 48, 99, 109, 112-13
St. John valley, upper 112
St. John watershed 90
St. John wilderness 89
St. John's tributaries 112
St. Lawrence River 13, 22, 30, 99
St. Lawrence valley 112
Steele, T. S. *Paddle and Portage* 108
Stevens, Thomas 57
Stillwater River xii
Stillwater, Maine 7
Sugar Island 80
Sunkhaze Stream 73
Sweeney Brook 98
Sweeny Brook 98
Swift River 58
Sysladobsis Lake 81

Index

Taconic 60
Taconic Falls 59
Taconic, "where they cross" 59
Tannery Brook 49
Telos 93
Telos Cut 93
The Allagash River 112
the Chops 59
The Forks
    Kennebec River 60, 63, 64, 115
The Northwest Carry House 65
The Woodpecker 11
Thibodeau Brook 107
Thoreau, Henry David xi,
    40, 43, 93, 115, 118
Thoroughfare Brook 110
Thurlotte, Jules 116, 118
Thurston Pond 72
thwarts 27
"ticook" 13
Tobique River 106
Toddy Pond 72
togue 8
tohque' ngau, paddle 28
Tomah, Sack (Jacques Thomas) 75, 78
Tomah Stream 90
Topsham 57
Trail of Tears, x
Treat, Joseph xi
Treats Falls 78
tumpline 28, 41
Tungus 21
Turner Farm 53
Twenty-Mile Stream 60
Twin Brook Falls 109

Udegeys 21
Umbazooksus, "much meadow" 97
Umbazooksus Stream 97, 115
umiak 21
Union 67
Union River 42, 49, 72-73
Union River, West Branch 81
Unity Pond 60
University of Maine 14, 73, 80
University of Maine, Orono 10

Veazie 72
Vermont 6
Verona Island xi, 72
Violette Brook 107

Wabanaki ix
Wabenobahntuk, "white water falls" 72
Wadleigh Deadwater 91
Wadleigh Pond 94
Walkers Pond 69
wangan 23
Wangan Brook 9
wangan, wanigan 9
Wassategwewick, "place where they spear
    fish" 91
Webster Stream 42, 93
weight-to-strength ratio 27
Weir Cove 69
Wesserunsett Stream 64
West Branch Archaeological Survey 96
West Branch Drive 5
Westerly, RI 19
Whale Cove 55
white cedar 27
White Mountains 56
white pine 16, 79
Whitefield 67
whitewater 64
Whiting's Hill 49
Whitten, Jeanne Patten 10
Wilson Street 11
Winnegance, "the carry" 59
Winnipesaukee, Lake 56
Winterport 72
Wiswell Hill 48
World War II 10, 65
Worromontogus Stream 59

Yakuts 21

David S. Cook grew up in the town of Milo, Maine. As a paratrooper in the U.S. Army's 101st Airborne Division, he served a tour of duty in South Vietnam. A graduate of the University of Maine, Orono, with a Master's degree in liberal studies, the author chose to live in Maine and taught history at Winthrop High School, where he was chairman of the Social Studies Department. He has served as president of the Maine Archeological Society, and since retiring has been an adjunct faculty member at Central Maine Community College and the University of Maine at Farmington, continuing to research and explore the history and ecology of Maine and the Northeast. David Cook is also the author of *History of the 3rd Maine Infantry Regiment* (Polar Bear & Company, 2017).

Photo Robert Edwards

www.ingramcontent.com/pod-product-compliance
Lightning Source LLC
LaVergne TN
LVHW041335080426
835512LV00006B/466